grand theft auto
Vice city

OFFICIAL STRATEGY guide

BY TIM BOGENN

table of contents

SONNY

Introduction

Somewhere along the sun-drenched coasts of Florida in the 1980s, there was a place called Vice City. Filled with drugs, gangsters, and a general populace ranging from extremely rich to very poor, it's a town filled with opportunities for the right kind of person.

Tommy Vercetti is just the type to take advantage of those opportunities. After being thrown in jail for 15 years and left to rot by his mob family, he's now out and looking to get back in the business. A trip south from Liberty City to do a simple transaction for the mob quickly gets out of hand. Tommy winds up without the money he was told to deliver, the coke he was supposed to pick up, or even any surviving members of his small group.

That's just about where you come in. There are cars to jack, missions to complete, jobs to do for people, sights to see, properties to purchase, extra (and fun) stuff to play around with, new weapons (even a few tools), a few changes of clothing, and many new acquaintances to meet—friends who can help you create your own criminal empire in Vice City.

Basics

This section gives you a broad overview of the contents of *Grand Theft Auto: Vice City*. We provide the details on some of the more basic mechanical aspects of the game, plus the various things you can do around town. If you're looking to get right into the heart of the matter, though, then check out our walkthrough strategy for the Main Story missions, as well as the Property Asset and Extra jobs. If you want to relax and mess around a bit, flip right to the Bonus Stuff chapter for specifics on the secret diversions hidden around the city.

CONTROLS

Setup 1 (default) In Car

L1	Change Radio Stations	**SELECT**	Camera Modes
L2	Look Left (+ Uzi and Circle = Drive-by)	▶	Pause Menu
R1	Hand Brake	RT ●	Turret Controls (Rhino)
R2	Look Right (+ Uzi and Circle = Drive-by)	**R3**	Begin Sub-mission
L2 + **R2**	Look Behind	△	Enter and Exit Vehicle
✛	Vehicle Control	○	Fire
LT ●	Vehicle Control/lean forward or back on bikes	✕	Accelerate
L3	Horn (Sirens or hydraulics when applicable)	▢	Brake/Reverse

Setup 1 (default) On Foot

L1	Look Forward	▶	Pause Menu
L2	Cycle Weapon Left	RT ●	1st Person Camera
R1	Target	**R3**	Look Behind
R2	Cycle Weapon Right	△	Enter Vehicles
✛	Movement	○	Attack
LT ●	Movement	✕	Run
L3	Crouch	▢	Jump
SELECT	Camera Modes		

WHAT'S NEW?

VEHICLES

Motorcycles! Yes, you can now cruise the streets on your own personal bike and pop a wheelie past the cop cars. These two-wheeled rides also provide the ability to fire straight ahead with certain weapons—something you cannot do in any car or truck.

You can even take to the air in Vice City. Fly helicopters and a seaplane. There are also several different types of new cars, as well as some new radio controlled vehicles.

There are some new opportunities and hazards, too. Tires can now be shot out. (Watch out, the police will deploy spike strips!) You can take out the driver of a vehicle with some accurate shooting. Control becomes increasingly difficult with each blown tire, and driving a vehicle with four blown tires is nearly impossible.

PROPERTY

You can purchase real estate around Vice City. Pick up a Save House of your choice. You'll get multiple garages, a place to save, and storage for all the goodies you've earned from collecting Hidden Packages at several locations. All Save House locations are available for purchase from the beginning of the game, except for those on the Mainland. These open after the "Phnom Penh '86" mission once the roadblocks have been removed.

You can also purchase certain pieces of real estate that have missions tied to them (indeed, you must to finish the main story). Very often, when you complete these missions, the property will begin to generate revenue for you, which you can cruise by and pick up any time. These are called Asset Properties.

WELCOME TO VICE CITY | MAIN STORY MISSIONS | EXTRA MISSIONS | ODD JOBS | BONUS STUFF

ASSET PROPERTIES

At the beginning of the game, the Asset Properties are not purchasable (indicated by the red house icon in front of them). The house icon turns green and the Properties become purchasable after completing "Shakedown" in Tommy's Protection Ring missions. You must perform certain tasks before certain Properties begin generating daily cash. These details are listed below.

Boatyard

The Boatyard in Viceport can be purchased for $10,000. Once "Checkpoint Charlie" is complete, it will generate $2000 max per day. Other benefits include free boats.

Cherry Popper Ice Cream Factory

The ice cream factory in Little Haiti costs $20,000. Once the Distribution mission that it unlocks is complete, it will generate $3000 max per day. Benefits include a Drug Distribution mission that provides a small reward per transaction.

Kaufman Cabs

This Little Haiti cab company costs $40,000, but once purchased, it will generate $5000 max per day and allow you to take the three Kaufman Cab missions. Complete these missions to unlock the Zebra Cab, which will appear in the Kaufman Cab building.

Car Showroom

Sunshine Autos in Little Havana costs $50,000. It generates $1500 a day per import/export board completed ($6000 in total), includes a free Pay 'n' Spray on the property, provides a Save House + four garages, and unlocks the Vice City Racer missions.

Print Works

Purchase the Print Works in Little Haiti for $70,000. Once its mission strand is complete, it will generate $8,000 max per day. Completing these missions is also a prerequisite to access the finale of the Main Story missions.

Film Studio

Purchase the Film Studio on Prawn Island for $60,000 and it will generate $7,000 max per day once its mission strand is complete.

The Malibu

The Malibu Club in Vice Point has a steep price of $100,000. However, once its mission strand is complete, it will generate $10,000 max per day. Owning this institute is a prerequisite to the finale.

Pole Position

The Pole Position in Washington Beach will set you back $30,000, but once you spend $600 on the dancer in first room in the open hallway, the property will generate $4000 max per day. Make sure you check out the room in the back of this hallway, as well!

SAVE HOUSE PROPERTIES

The following are non-Asset properties that can be purchased from the beginning of the game and after "Shakedown" (Mainland Properties). Save your progress at these locations using the Save Tape. You can also store your vehicles at some.

Elswanko Casa

Costs $8000, has one garage, and is located in Vice Point, south of the North Point Mall and east of Leaf Links north island.

Links View Apartments

Costs $6000, has one garage, and is located east of Leaf Links Island and west of the Vice Point Police Station.

Ocean Heights

Costs $7000, has one garage, and is located on the southernmost block in Ocean Beach.

Hyman Condo

Costs $14,000, has three garages and one Helipad, and is located on the block east of Hyman Memorial Stadium (Mainland).

1102 Washington Street

Costs $3000 and is located across from Ken Rosenberg's office in Washington Beach.

3321 Vice Point

Costs $2500 and is located on the shoreline north of North Point Mall.

Skumole Shack

Costs $1000 and is located Downtown, on a rooftop that's down the street and around the corner north of the Biker Bar.

WHEELIES, STOPPIES, AND TWO WHEEL BONUSES

You will see Wheelies, Stoppies, and Two Wheel bonuses on the Stats menu. The Two Wheel challenge is done in any four-wheel vehicle. See how long you can maintain a vehicle on its side while riding on two wheels! Bonuses are awarded for beating your own best time for all these tricks. Use any Motorcycle to pull off a Wheelie. Pull back on the Control Stick, gas it up, and then ride it out as long as you can. The Stoppie is performed on any two-wheeled cycle, except the Harley-type bikes. Reach a maximum speed on the cycle, then press both brakes (hand and regular brakes) at the same time while leaning forward. Lean forward and backward to maintain the balance and see how long you can hold the Stoppie.

ROBBING SHOPS

You can knock over some Vice City shops for cash and a piece of the 100% completion of the game! Simply walk into one of the following shops, then target (but don't shoot) the cashier, and he'll promptly fork over cash. The longer you hold your aim, the more money he coughs up, until three stacks of cash have been dispensed. Shoot him before letting up your aim and he won't hit the alarm. Either way, the cops will be on the way, so get out of there quickly!

STORE TO ROB	LOCATION
Corner Store	Vice Point, one block north of the Shady Points Hospital.
Dispensary + (Pharmacy)	Vice Point, one block west of the Corner Store.
Jewelry Store	Vice Point, just east of bridge to Leaf Links Country Club.
Gash	North Point Mall
Music Store	North Point Mall
Jewelry Store	North Point Mall
Hardware Store	North Point Mall
Bunch of Tools (Hardware)	Washington Beach, on peninsula west of Washington Beach Police Department.
Ryton Aide Pharmacy	Little Haiti, next to Pay 'n' Spray.
Pharmacy	Downtown, on the street between Love Fist's Studio and Rock City.
Jewelry Store	Downtown, on the street between Love Fist's Studio and Rock City.
Deli	Little Havana, one street north of Ryton Aide.
Doughnut Shop	Little Havana, on the corner south of Cherry Popper.
Laundromat	Little Havana, west of the Print Works.
Screw This (Hardware)	Little Havana, between Umberto's and Sunshine Autos.

CLOTHING STORES

There are 10 different outfits that can be worn anytime after unlocking them. The following is a list of Tommy's growing wardrobe and where they are located.

Street Outfit

Unlocked after completing "An Old Friend" (Rosenberg mission). It is delivered to each Save House after their purchase, including Tommy's Estate (after the "Rub Out" mission).

Soiree Outfit

Unlocked after "The Party" (Rosenberg mission). It is delivered to Rafael's.

Coveralls

Unlocked after "Riot" (Rosenberg mission). It is delivered to Tooled Up in the North Point Mall.

Country Club Outfit

Unlocked after "Four Iron" (Avery Carrington mission). It is delivered to the Golf Club.

Havana Outfit

Unlocked after "Two Bit Hit" (Avery Carrington mission). It is delivered to Little Havana Streetwear.

Cop Outfit

Unlocked after "Cop Land" (Protection Ring mission). It is delivered to the Police Station in Washington Beach.

Bank Job Outfit

Unlocked after "The Job" (Malibu mission). It is delivered to the Malibu Club in Vice Point.

Casual Outfit

Unlocked after "Treacherous Swine" (Colonel mission). It is delivered to the Gash in North Point Mall.

Mr. Vercetti Outfit

Unlocked after buying the Pole Position and is delivered to Collar & Cuffs.

Tracksuit

Unlocked after "Supply and Demand" (Diaz mission). It is delivered to Jocksport in Downtown.

WHAT'S NEW?

100% COMPLETION

To reach 100% completion (indicated on the stats menu), you must complete all of the following challenges:

- All Main Story Missions
- All Extra Missions
- All Odd Jobs
- All Rampages
- All Unique Jumps
- Collect 100 Hidden Packages
- Purchase All Properties
- Rob All Stores

EXTRA MISSIONS

In addition to the missions tied to real estate, there are also several Extra missions—everything from Helicopter checkpoint races to a demolition derby arena.

OTHER GOODIES

Building interiors are accessible (including a large mall to explore). Inside areas are key locations for many missions, as well as for some less obvious purposes—like buying food to gain health.

The map in Vice City is very tight. You'll find the in-game map especially handy for finding your way around town.

There are gang wars in Vice City, but you can save the Cuban or Haitian missions until attempting full completion of the game, so you won't have to deal with quite so many random people on the streets gunning for you.

Vice City's targeting system makes combat on foot very manageable. If you're a type that usually has a hard time aiming, you'll find it easy to deal with in this town.

There's also a large arsenal of weapons, including nasty new melee weapons like the chainsaw, and an impressive array of shotguns, assault rifles, submachine guns, and more. (See the Weapons section of this guide for all the details.)

CRIME AND PUNISHMENT

There are lots of ways to find trouble in Vice City, but only a few ways out—usually involving jail or a pine box.

WANTED LEVEL

Any illicit activities you perform while out in public have the potential of arousing police interest. This is measured by your Wanted Level, which ranges from one star, all the way up to six. Get it to five and the FBI becomes involved. Reach six and the military shows up to terminate you.

As soon as your Wanted Level exceeds a single star, the law pursues you relentlessly until you take steps to remove some stars. A single star, however, will elapse on its own over time, as long as you don't get into any more trouble.

SHAKING THE HEAT

There are a few ways to reduce your Wanted Level. You can find Police Bribes scattered around the city (see our Police Bribes map in the Bonus Stuff section of this guide); picking one up lowers your level by one star.

Clean Duds
Changing clothes will clear a 1- or 2-star Wanted Level.

Another option is to drive into a Pay 'n' Spray. This not only fixes your car, but also completely clears your Wanted Level. However, there is a catch here—your current stars will briefly remain flashing when you emerge with your shiny new paint job. If you do anything illegal during this time, your Wanted Level will be fully reinstated. Keep that in mind if you just made a narrow escape from the military and some guy cuts you off in his moped. It's probably not worth it.

Of course there are also the less pleasant ways out of trouble. If you bite it (either by losing your health, getting caught inside an exploding vehicle, or falling in the water), you'll wake up at the nearest Hospital, sans weaponry and minus a bit of cash.

If you get busted by a cop or the FBI, you'll wind up at the local Police Station; again, minus your weapons and cash. The military has no interest in busting you; they'll simply blast you.

You must now also be wary of the cops on foot—they will open your car door and bust you much quicker than they did in Liberty City. Perhaps there's better training in Vice City.

WANTED LEVEL BREAKDOWN

The following is what to expect from Vice City heat.

This is a low-level alert; any cop on foot or in a passing cruiser will follow you. If they pull you out of a car or knock you down to the ground, you're busted. Find one Bribe or lay low for a while to shake this minor offense. The police carry Colt 45s and Nightsticks.

Things heat up a bit with the second star. Expect to see two cruisers in hot pursuit. The cops may even shoot first and read you your rights later. You cannot simply shake this level of trouble, so visit a Pay 'n' Spray or find some Police Bribes to get the law off your back.

Reminiscent of Crockett and Tubbs from Miami Vice (packing Uzi 9mms), new heat join the chase in their Cheetah, while a helicopter serves as the eye-in-the-sky. Light roadblocks, comprised of one or two cruisers, also appear to barricade major streets.

Police cruisers arrive quickly and violently, the helicopter never pauses to take a shot at you, Tire Strips are pushed out onto the roads, and SWAT teams in Enforcers jump into the action (packing Uzis and Colt 45s). If they catch you, the bamboo under the fingernail treatment is likely. Also watch out for SWAT troops roping out of helicopters.

Five stars merits all the heat of the previous alert with the addition of the FBI in their black Ranchers! There are four FBI agents in each SUV, and they all pile out and begin shooting upon arrival. FBI agents carry MP5s and Colt 45s.

The Army is called into action when you reach the maximum Wanted Level. Soldiers in Rhinos, Barrack OLs, and flatbeds flood the streets, carrying MP5s, Grenades, and Colt 45s. The helicopter still buzzes overhead. You're in deep now, buddy!

GETTING AROUND

ON FOOT

Yes, it's true, you'll occasionally have to give up your lead foot and hike around the city. There are many good reasons to do this: You can access areas difficult or impossible to reach in vehicles, fighting is easier with all of your available weapons, and you can escape pursuit more easily.

Also, fairly obviously, being on foot is your ticket to a new vehicle. Jacking a car is simple, and you're limited only by what happens to be around when you want a new ride.

Running improves your endurance over the course of the game. Tommy initially wears out fairly quickly, but is eventually able to travel great distances at a good clip on foot. This is pretty handy in more than a few situations.

Using weapons while on foot is also important or necessary in some missions, and it's quite useful when you want to destroy a vehicle quicker than simply ramming it with something that weighs more.

CRUISING THE STREETS

Vehicles are at the heart of the game—they're everywhere. There are boats at the docks, helicopters on landing pads, and cars and motorcycles all over the city, just waiting for your tender ministrations (or mid-traffic carjackings and rampant abuse, whichever you prefer).

Taxi Rides

A mysterious Kaufman Cab shows up outside of the Hospital or Police Station after being Busted or getting Wasted on a mission. Enter the cab with the large arrow above it, and for a mere $9, it will whisk you to the location where you picked up the job you failed. It's a cool little feature that gets you back on the job quicker.

The Bail Out

Remember that any vehicle you drive can suffer from damage, including having its tires destroyed, so watch the smoke to know when you need to bail out. If the smoke is white, you're still okay, but be careful once it's black. If your vehicle starts flaming, get out immediately and run for cover!

It's also possible to do a diving bail out, which means you can use cars as giant mobile explosives if you feel the need. To bail out of a vehicle, you need Speed + Triangle.

Garages

If you find a vehicle that you particularly like, take it to one of your garages and store it. If you have several Save Houses, then you can store multiple vehicles. It's handy to have a variety of rides around when you need a specific kind (fast cars for some missions, more durable trucks or vans for others).

Motorcycle Drive-bys

Keep in mind that motorcycles make better gun platforms than most other vehicles. You can shoot forward on a bike, which enables you to chase down targets and destroy their vehicle from behind— something you can't do while shooting out the side windows of the other vehicles.

Earliest Chopper

The earliest you can take to the Vice City skies is immediately after the roads blocks are removed, allowing you access to the mainland. This happens during "Sir, Yes, Sir" (Colonel's Missions). Provided that you've done a lot of side work and have $14,000 burning a hole in your pocket, purchase the Hyman Condo (near Hyman Stadium in north Downtown) for the said amount, then enter via the roof access door near the Save Tape. On the rooftop, you'll find a helipad with your very own Maverick!

Weapons

Ah, yes... the tools of rampant mayhem and abuse. There are plenty of guns in Vice City—ranging from the very impressive and high-powered chaingun, down to the more modest and familiar pistol.

You can carry several weapons around with you (multiple light weapons and a single heavy weapon), so find the ones you like and carry them with you. Several of the larger or more powerful weapons prevent you from running while they're active, so make sure you holster them if you need to get somewhere quickly.

Your weapons are essential for certain missions, and useful for quickly destroying vehicles in many others. If you are going to hop out of your car and shoot at a vehicle, be sure that you've blocked them off or trapped them; otherwise, your target may vanish before you can draw a bead.

You can carry nine different categories of weapons (10 if you count the camera). We refer to them as weapon placement "slots." To change weapons (moving the slots), press the L2 and R2 Buttons. The following is a list and description of every weapon found in Vice City.

CAMERA (SLOT 1)

In the first available weapon slot, Tommy holds the Camera. When you do not have the Camera, Slot 1 disappears and Slot 2 becomes the first Slot.

CAMERA
Only available in the "Martha's Mug Shot" mission, the camera is used to capture and frame a congressman engaged in an indecent act.

FIST OF STEEL (SLOT 2)

The second weapon slot is dedicated to your fists and to the Brass Knuckles. If you don't have the Brass Knuckles, you'll be fighting with your own flesh-and-bone fists. This slot cannot be used to hold any other weapon.

BRASS KNUCKLES
These linked metal rings with holes for the fingers are worn for rough fighting. This variety is actually made with Steel. Bouncers at The Malibu carry them. They can also be found as a weapon pick-up behind the Moonlight Hotel on Ocean Drive.

MELEE WEAPONS/CHAINSAW (SLOT 3)

In the third weapon slot, Tommy can hold only one of the following melee weapons. These are your home improvement, pummeling, jabbing, and general slice-n-dice weapons. They are immediately available for purchase in the game from Tool shops.

SCREW DRIVER
Use this for turning screws or creating gaping holes in your targets.

HAMMER
Ordinarily used to pound or pull nails, you'll likely pummel thugs with this tool in Vice City.

GOLF CLUB
Primarily used for sport, especially if that sport involves wrapping a club around the neck of someone you don't particularly like. Get them from golfers on Leaf Links Island and from the Leaf Links Country Club.

NIGHTSTICK
The policeman's billy club, Nightsticks are great for breaking into cars and pounding skulls. Steal them from cops or acquire them inside police stations.

BASEBALL BAT

This is the conventional thrashing device in Vice City. Buy them from Tool shops after completing Rosenberg's third job, "Jury Fury."

KNIFE

In Vice City, this single-edged sharp blade is used for cutting and stabbing thugs, not food. Purchase Knives from Tool shops after completing Rosenberg's second job, "Back Alley Brawl." You can also pick up a free Knife behind the Northstar Hotel on Ocean Drive.

CLEAVER

The Cleaver is a heavy cutting tool with a broad blade, used by butchers—and Tommy Vercetti. They're available for purchase from the start of the game at any Tool shop. Get one at no cost behind the north pizza restaurant.

MACHETE

The Machete is a large, heavy-bladed knife that's usually used for cutting down dense underbrush; however, it can also be used to shorten tall people. The bartender at the Pole Position Club carries one of these. You can also buy them in Tool shops after completing Rosenberg's third job, "Jury Fury."

KATANA

The Katana is an Asian Ninja sword with a long, curved, single-edged blade. Press and hold the Circle Button to carry this weapon above your head, then release the button to swing. During combat combinations, you can run someone through, killing them instantly. Purchase Katanas from Tool shops, or find one free at the Tarbrush Café in North Point Mall. There's also one in Diaz's next-door neighbor's garage on Starfish Island.

CHAINSAW

The Chainsaw is a portable power tool with a rotating chain of cutting teeth. Aside from its traditional association with lumber tasks, this tool can be used for making a bloody mess out of anyone that stands in your way.

PROJECTILES (SLOT 4)

Weapon slot four is reserved for the thrown explosives category. Press and hold the Circle Button, then release it to toss the projectile of choice. The longer you hold the button down, the farther the throw. You cannot run and throw projectiles at the same time.

GRENADES

These small bombs detonate within a certain amount of time after leaving the user's hand. Great for destroying vehicles and stopping large crowds, you can eventually purchase grenades from Ammu-Nation, or get free ones from the Basketball court near the Ice Cream Factory.

MOLOTOV

A Molotov is a bottle filled with gasoline and plugged with a saturated rag for a wick. This bomb is ignited and hurled as a poor man's grenade. Persons or objects hit by this weapon will begin to burn, causing firefighters to respond. Molotovs are available only at the Taco Shop downtown—must be the secret to their hot sauce.

TEARGAS

This volatile gas canister causes irritation of the eyes, a heavy flow of tears, and temporary blindness. Teargas is usually used in warfare or by the police. Persons caught in the cloud will first lose their armor, and then their health. Find this weapon outside the Beach police station.

BOMB/DETONATOR

The bomb and detonator is nothing more than a regular grenade with a detonation device. Throw the bomb as you would any projectile weapon, then press the Circle Button again (the detonator will appear in the weapon slot once the bomb leaves your hand) to detonate the bomb. This gives you plenty of time to get away from the blast. You can buy these at Phil's Place once you've acquired the property.

PISTOL (SLOT 5)

The pistol slot allows you to carry one of the following handguns.

COLT 45

Used by the U.S. Army for over 80 years, this durable pistol has a heavy slide and bolt that slams back and forth with each shot. Expect less accurate hits than those you'll get with the Python. You can buy Colt 45s from the start of the game at Ammu-Nation.

COLT PYTHON

This elite, double action, swing-out cylinder revolver has a 6-inch barrel and fires .357 magnum rounds. The length of the barrel translates into incredible accuracy and one-hit kills. You can buy them at Ammu-Nation after the "Rub Out" mission. You cannot walk or run when shooting this revolver.

SHOTGUN (SLOT 6)

Slot 6 is for carrying one of the following shotguns. You cannot run while firing shotguns.

CHROMED SHOTGUN

Double the barrels, double the fun… This chrome-plated beauty offers extreme damage to near-by targets. Purchase this weapon from the main-land Ammu-Nation or get a free one at the top of the Washington Mall.

SPAZ SHOTGUN

The double barrel Spaz Shotgun offers seven quick-fire shell shots before pausing for reload. If you want a free one, look across from the main terminal at the airport.

STUBBY SHOTGUN

This little sawed-off shotgun is available for pur-chase at the Ammu-Nation in North Point Mall. Look for the weapon pick-up behind the large hangar near the Junkyard.

UZI (SLOT 7)

Only one of the following Uzis can be held at a time, and only the Tec9 and the Uzi 9mm can be fired while running. Holding down the Circle Button for long periods of time to shoot decreases your accuracy, so let up from time to time to fire again—you'll score more hits.

TEC-9

Criminals can easily convert the infa-mous and inexpensive TEC-9 to full-auto; this has caused the weapon to acquire a notorious reputation in the U.S. Find Tec-9s on the small road that leads to the golf course.

INGRAM MAC 10

Developed by Gordon Ingram at his Military Armament Company (MAC), the Mac 10 is a recoil-operated, select-fire submachine gun. Its light weight and high rate of fire result in marginal accuracy and a relatively short effective range.

UZI 9MM

This ergonomic submachine gun has its magazine housing inside the pistol grip, making it easier to reload in tight situations. Find this Uzi behind the Pay 'n' Spray in Washington, across from the Biker Bar. There's another one in front of the thugs' hangout on Prawn Island.

MP5

The MP5 submachine gun utilizes a delayed blowback technology—this variety of weapons provides a greater degree of accuracy. Numerous military and law enforcement units in more than 60 nations use the MP5, firmly establishing the MP5 as the world's most recognizable submachine gun. You can fill Slot 7 with an MP5 if you're good enough to take one from an FBI agent.

ASSAULT RIFLES (SLOT 8)

The Ruger and the M4 have one thing in common: they can both be fired in rapid succession while using their sighting systems (R1 Button). Neither can be fired while running.

RUGER

This rifle is found during the third Cuban job and the third job for the Colonel. It excels as a deadly distant shooter, as well as a close combat weapon. If you don't have a sniper rifle, don't sweat it—this one will do the job.

COLT M4

Intended for use by Special Operations forces and other select members of the military, the Colt M4 is now available to criminals in Vice City. The M4 has full-auto capabilities and a sighting system. These deadly weapons are found in the slums of Little Haiti, behind a house near Umberto's Café in Little Havana, in the basement of your Mansion, and inside Studio B on Prawn Island.

HEAVY METAL (SLOT 9)

Tommy can hold only one of the following implements of mass destruction at a time. These weapons are heavy, so expect very slow movement when armed with one.

ROCKET LAUNCHER

It's pretty self-explanatory: it launches rockets. Just don't stand too close to the target or you'll become part of the mess. Buy them at Phil's Place once you've acquired that property. Also, look for one cooling off in the pool of the Hooker Inn (near the airport).

FLAME-THROWER

Yes, indeed... this weapon throws flames. Avoid running into an area that has been engulfed in flames and don't touch the burning victims as they run frantically from the inferno. The Flame-thrower is found right out in the open, alongside a south road in the Docks area of Viceport. There's another one in an unlikely place: the Rock Star pool on Starfish Island.

M60

The Army's general-purpose machine gun, which entered service in the 1950s, is lightweight and easy to carry considering its size—it's meant to be operated by two soldiers. Buy one at Phil's Place, or be adventurous and find the one in the left tower at Fort Baxter Air Base.

MINIGUN

Better known as the Gattling Gun, the Minigun was declared obsolete by the U.S. Army in 1911 after 45 years of service to the Army. The advent of the automatic machine gun put it out of service, but with your help, it will reach the top of the ranks again, here in Vice City. Purchase Mini Guns at Phil's Place after acquiring his estate.

SNIPER: SLOT 10

There are two sniping weapons, and only one can be held in Slot 10 at a time.

SNIPER RIFLE

This is a single shot rifle with a scope. It's slow on the reload, but gets the job done. You can buy it at an Ammu-Nation or pick one up from Diaz's maze, outside his mansion. There's another behind the tollbooth on the last bridge to the beach from the mainland.

PSG-1

The PSG-1 disproves the widespread prejudice that optimal firing accuracy can be achieved only with single loaders. The PSG-1 is said to be the most accurate semi-auto in the world. Find one next to the Kaufman Cab billboard in Little Havana (near Umberto's Café) or purchase it from the Downtown Ammu-Nation for an arm and a leg (try Phil's arm).

ITEMS

A variety of pickups are scattered about Vice City to help you in a variety of ways.

HEALTH

Grab this little heart to restore your vitality to 100. If you expect to be involved in a dangerous situation and you're only slightly dinged up, save this power-up for the middle of the conflict. Better to get 90 health out of it than just 10.

BODY ARMOR

Body Armor provides 100 points of protection on top of your 100 health, making you a much more durable target. Pick up a suit of this every time you begin a mission, either at an Ammu-Nation or one from around town.

ADRENALINE

Adrenaline can get you through some very difficult situations without a scratch. It gives you the strength to push cars and slows the rest of the world to a crawl. Try it in combination with different weapons to see how you can best use it.

POLICE BRIBES

These drop your Wanted Level by a single star, which may not seem like too much until you consider the marked difference between the higher Wanted Levels.

RAMPAGES

Grab one of these Skull icons to initiate a mini mission. Typically, these involve causing some specific type of mayhem within a limited time span. Don't worry if you fail, you can always find the Rampage icon later and attempt it again.

Vehicle Showroom

Whether you're looking for a two-door compact, speedboat, motorcycle, helicopter, or even a garbage truck, you've come to the right place! We have everything you need for a low, low price. We're Diversified Dealers!

Actually, everything's free.

The following is a virtual showroom of every available vehicle in Vice City.

Vice City Rides
You'll be able to quickly find high performance vehicles or muscle cars without too much trouble. If it's late in the day, look inside the carparks near each mall—you're sure to find some nice rides there if the streets are empty.

2-DOOR & MUSCLE CARS

BLISTA COMPACT

Cool Factor:	●●●●●○○○○○
Speed:	●●●●●○○○○○
Handling:	●●●●●●○○○○
Cornering:	●●●●●●○○○○

FEATURES & COMMENTS
Small, light, and low to the ground, this puppy scoots. If you see one of these, take it!

CUBAN HERMES

Cool Factor:	●●●●●●●●●○
Speed:	●●●●●●○○○○
Handling:	●●●●●○○○○○
Cornering:	●●●●○○○○○○

FEATURES & COMMENTS
It has a flame paint job. What more could you want?

HERMES

Cool Factor:	●●●●●●●●○○
Speed:	●●●●●●●○○○
Handling:	●●●●●○○○○○
Cornering:	●●●●●○○○○○

FEATURES & COMMENTS
Gas it up to speed and press the L3 Button for an aerial spectacle you've just got to see!

MANANA

Cool Factor:	●●●○○○○○○○
Speed:	●●●●○○○○○○
Handling:	●●●○○○○○○○
Cornering:	●●●●○○○○○○

FEATURES & COMMENTS
Cooler than driving a Trashmaster. Actually, this car is not a bad ride if nothing else is around.

PHOENIX

Cool Factor:
Speed:
Handling:
Cornering:

FEATURES & COMMENTS
This is a great car. If you have a mullet, you'll enjoy it even more!

SABRE TURBO

Cool Factor:
Speed:
Handling:
Cornering:

FEATURES & COMMENTS
Similar to the normal Sabre, only this one is quicker on the get-up-and-go.

SABRE

Cool Factor:
Speed:
Handling:
Cornering:

FEATURES & COMMENTS
The Sabre has lots of horsepower, a low center of gravity, and decent cornering ability.

STALLION

Cool Factor:
Speed:
Handling:
Cornering:

FEATURES & COMMENTS
Not as cool as the Sabre, but it's a classic.

VOODOO

Cool Factor:
Speed:
Handling:
Cornering:

FEATURES & COMMENTS
This is one bad ghetto cruiser! Press the L3 Button for hydraulic lift and lowering; use the Right Analog Stick for left, right, forward, and rear hydraulics. ...And she was SHAKING!

AIRCRAFT

MAVERICK

Cool Factor:
Speed:
Handling:
Cornering:

FEATURES & COMMENTS
Great for getting around town—or over town.

POLICE MAVERICK

Cool Factor:
Speed:
Handling:
Cornering:

FEATURES & COMMENTS
This is a law enforcement aircraft, but without weapons and no Vigilante mode.

SEA SPARROW

Cool Factor:
Speed:
Handling:
Cornering:

FEATURES & COMMENTS
Not only is this a thrill to fly, it also shoots when you press the R1 Button and floats on water!

SKIMMER

Cool Factor:
Speed:
Handling:
Cornering:

FEATURES & COMMENTS
This is no Dodo!

SPARROW

Cool Factor:	●●●●●●●○○○○○○○○
Speed:	●●●●●●●●○○○○○○○
Handling:	●●●○○○○○○○○○○○○
Cornering:	●●●○○○○○○○○○○○○

FEATURES & COMMENTS
This is the choice whirly for all Chopper Checkpoint Challenges.

VCN MAVERICK

Cool Factor:	●●●●●●●●○○○○○○○
Speed:	●●●●●○○○○○○○○○○
Handling:	●●●●○○○○○○○○○○○
Cornering:	●●●●●●●●○○○○○○○

FEATURES & COMMENTS
A Maverick that is über-fast, but more sensitive during rolls. It is owned by a Vice City News organization.

BOATS

COAST GUARD

Cool Factor:	●●●●●○○○○○○○○○○
Speed:	●●●●●○○○○○○○○○○
Handling:	●●●●○○○○○○○○○○○
Cornering:	●●●○○○○○○○○○○○○

FEATURES & COMMENTS
A water peacekeeper, but it's not your boat for Vigilantes.

CUBAN JETMAX

Cool Factor:	●●●●●●○○○○○○○○○
Speed:	●●●●●●○○○○○○○○○
Handling:	●●●●●○○○○○○○○○○
Cornering:	●●○○○○○○○○○○○○○

FEATURES & COMMENTS
If you live after jacking one of these, you won't regret the risk involved.

DINGHY

Cool Factor:	●●●○○○○○○○○○○○○
Speed:	●●●●○○○○○○○○○○○
Handling:	●●●●○○○○○○○○○○○
Cornering:	●●●○○○○○○○○○○○○

FEATURES & COMMENTS
The Dinghy can be spotted during watery Wanted Levels, but you cannot initiate any Vigilante missions from this craft.

MARQUIS

Cool Factor:	●●●●●●●○○○○○○○○
Speed:	●●●●●○○○○○○○○○○
Handling:	●●●●○○○○○○○○○○○
Cornering:	●●●●○○○○○○○○○○○

FEATURES & COMMENTS
This is why you came to Vice City: to get away!

REEFER

Cool Factor:	●●●●○○○○○○○○○○○
Speed:	●●●●○○○○○○○○○○○
Handling:	●●●●○○○○○○○○○○○
Cornering:	●○○○○○○○○○○○○○○

FEATURES & COMMENTS
Great for dragging nets or getting your leg chomped by an enormous shark.

RIO

Cool Factor:	●●●●●●●●○○○○○○○
Speed:	●●●●○○○○○○○○○○○
Handling:	●●●●○○○○○○○○○○○
Cornering:	●●●○○○○○○○○○○○○

FEATURES & COMMENTS
…And when she shines, she really shows you all she can. Oh, Rio, Rio… dance across the Rio Grande!

SPEEDER

Cool Factor:	●●●●●●●○○○○○○○○
Speed:	●●●●●○○○○○○○○○○
Handling:	●●●●●○○○○○○○○○○
Cornering:	●●○○○○○○○○○○○○○

FEATURES & COMMENTS
Good speed for a boat, but cornering is a skill you must learn.

SQUALLO

Cool Factor:	●●●●●●●●○○○○○○○
Speed:	●●●●●●●●○○○○○○○
Handling:	●●●●○○○○○○○○○○○
Cornering:	●●●●○○○○○○○○○○○

FEATURES & COMMENTS
Double outboard nautical excitement. Comes standard with spare cement shoes for your late-night boating adventures.

TROPIC

Cool Factor:	●●●●●●●●○○
Speed:	●●●●●○○○○○
Handling:	●●●○○○○○○○
Cornering:	●●○○○○○○○○

FEATURES & COMMENTS
Get away… just leave the mainland for a while and take it easy.

HIGH PERFORMANCE

BANSHEE

Cool Factor:	●●●●●●●●○○
Speed:	●●●●●●●●○○
Handling:	●●●●●●●●○○
Cornering:	●●●●●●●○○○

FEATURES & COMMENTS
Not exactly rare, but you won't be complaining once you're behind the wheel!

BLOODRING BANGER

Cool Factor:	●●●●●●●●○○
Speed:	●●●●●●●○○○
Handling:	●●●●●○○○○○
Cornering:	●●●●○○○○○○

FEATURES & COMMENTS
Takes a lickin' and keeps on kickin'. Enter the Bloodring challenge at the Arena after 8pm and get behind the wheel of a Banger for some demolition derby delight!

CHEETAH

Cool Factor:	●●●●●●●●●○
Speed:	●●●●●●●●○○
Handling:	●●●●●●○○○○
Cornering:	●●●●●●●○○○

FEATURES & COMMENTS
Jack one of these during a Wanted Level 3, then trigger the Vigilante Missions from inside by pressing the R3 Button. Bust the bad guys in style!

COMET

Cool Factor:	●●●●●●●●●○
Speed:	●●●●●●●●○○
Handling:	●●●●●●●●○○
Cornering:	●●●●●●●●○○

FEATURES & COMMENTS
The Comet is fast and handles well, but it's also very fragile.

DELUXO

Cool Factor:	●●●●●●●●●○
Speed:	●●●●●●●○○○
Handling:	●●●●●●●○○○
Cornering:	●●●●●●●●○○

FEATURES & COMMENTS
Going back in time… this is one of Vice City's coolest cars!

HOTRING RACER

Cool Factor:	●●●●●●●○○○
Speed:	●●●●●●●●●○
Handling:	●●●●●●●○○○
Cornering:	●●●●●●○○○○

FEATURES & COMMENTS
Handbrake cornering is key to moving ahead of the pack in the Hotring. Collect the cars needed for the Showroom's fourth garage and you could be driving this on the streets of Vice City!

STINGER

Cool Factor:	●●●●●●●○○○
Speed:	●●●●●●●○○○
Handling:	●●●●●●●●○○
Cornering:	●●●●●●●●○○

FEATURES & COMMENTS
This is the ultimate ride for cruising the beach. It's an awesome convertible sports car! Chicks dig it.

INFERNUS

Cool Factor:	●●●●●●●●●○
Speed:	●●●●●●●●○○
Handling:	●●●●●●●○○○
Cornering:	●●●●●●●●○○

FEATURES & COMMENTS
Who's bad?!

MIDSIZE

ADMIRAL

Cool Factor:	●●●●○○○○○○○○
Speed:	●●●●●○○○○○○○
Handling:	●●●●●○○○○○○○
Cornering:	●●●●●○○○○○○○

FEATURES & COMMENTS
A well rounded, old, luxury 4-door.

ESPERANTO

Cool Factor:	●●●○○○○○○○○○
Speed:	●●●●○○○○○○○○
Handling:	●●●●○○○○○○○○
Cornering:	●●●●○○○○○○○○

FEATURES & COMMENTS
This two-door midsize is a great car if you like fishing or robbing liquor stores.

GLENDALE

Cool Factor:	●●●●○○○○○○○○
Speed:	●●●●●○○○○○○○
Handling:	●●●●●○○○○○○○
Cornering:	●●●●●○○○○○○○

FEATURES & COMMENTS
Not a bad ride... Jack one today!

GREENWOOD

Cool Factor:	●●○○○○○○○○○○
Speed:	●●●●●●○○○○○○
Handling:	●●●●●○○○○○○○
Cornering:	●●●●●○○○○○○○

FEATURES & COMMENTS
The four-door version of the Virgo.

IDAHO

Cool Factor:	●●○○○○○○○○○○
Speed:	●●●○○○○○○○○○
Handling:	●●●●○○○○○○○○
Cornering:	●●●●○○○○○○○○

FEATURES & COMMENTS
It's a big beater, but has only two doors. What were the manufacturers smoking?

OCEANIC

Cool Factor:	●●●○○○○○○○○○
Speed:	●●●●○○○○○○○○
Handling:	●●●●○○○○○○○○
Cornering:	●●●●○○○○○○○○

FEATURES & COMMENTS
A classic!

PERENNIAL

Cool Factor:	●○○○○○○○○○○○
Speed:	●●●○○○○○○○○○
Handling:	●●●●○○○○○○○○
Cornering:	●●●○○○○○○○○○

FEATURES & COMMENTS
It has the paranormal ability to make anyone who enters it wish they had a minivan.

REGINA

Cool Factor:	●○○○○○○○○○○○
Speed:	●●●●○○○○○○○○
Handling:	●●●●○○○○○○○○
Cornering:	●●●○○○○○○○○○

FEATURES & COMMENTS
Nicer than the Perennial, but still a station wagon.

SENTINEL XS

Cool Factor:	●●●●●●○○○○○○
Speed:	●●●●●●○○○○○○
Handling:	●●●●●●○○○○○○
Cornering:	●●●●●●○○○○○○

FEATURES & COMMENTS
Not as flashy as some of the higher-performance vehicles, but this import has good speed and handling.

SENTINEL

Cool Factor:	●●●○○○○○○○○○
Speed:	●●●●○○○○○○○○
Handling:	●●●●○○○○○○○○
Cornering:	●●●●○○○○○○○○

FEATURES & COMMENTS
The average car for the average Joe.

VIRGO

Cool Factor:	●●
Speed:	●●●●
Handling:	●●●●
Cornering:	●●●●

FEATURES & COMMENTS

This two-door midsize vehicle is a notch above average.

WASHINGTON

Cool Factor:	●●●
Speed:	●●●●
Handling:	●●●●
Cornering:	●●●●

FEATURES & COMMENTS

Not as cool as the Washington those FBI guys are driving, but keep dreaming.

MISCELLANEOUS

BAGGAGE HANDLER

Cool Factor:	●
Speed:	●●●
Handling:	●●●●●
Cornering:	●●●●●

FEATURES & COMMENTS

Although it's a very interesting addition to the series, you probably still don't want to use it as a getaway car. However, it's still handy if you're stuck at the airport without a ride.

LOVE FIST

Cool Factor:	●●●●●●●●
Speed:	●●●●●
Handling:	●●●●
Cornering:	●●●●

FEATURES & COMMENTS

Lots of fun, except for the ticking bomb and the whining rock stars.

CADDY

Cool Factor:	●●●●●●●
Speed:	●●
Handling:	●●●●●
Cornering:	●●●●●

FEATURES & COMMENTS

The best mode of transportation on the greens—the only mode if you're in Bath, NC!

ROMERO'S HEARSE

Cool Factor:	●●●●●●
Speed:	●●●●●
Handling:	●●●●
Cornering:	●●●●

FEATURES & COMMENTS

A little stiff in the rear, but still handles pretty well.

STRETCH

Cool Factor:	●●●●●●
Speed:	●●●●
Handling:	●●●
Cornering:	●●

FEATURES & COMMENTS

This ride is at its coolest when you're not the chauffeur.

MOTORCYCLES

ANGEL

Cool Factor:	●●●●
Speed:	●●●●●
Handling:	●●●●
Cornering:	●●●

FEATURES & COMMENTS

Not much for speed and handling, but that's not why you ride it. Try to do a wheelie or a stoppie in a Cheetah!

FAGGIO

Cool Factor:	●●●●●●○○○○
Speed:	●○○○○○○○○○
Handling:	●●●○○○○○○○
Cornering:	●●●●○○○○○○

FEATURES & COMMENTS
Man, get off that thing before someone sees you! Although, this is your only choice if you have a DUI.

PCJ 600

Cool Factor:	●●●●●●●○○○
Speed:	●●●●●○○○○○
Handling:	●●●●○○○○○○
Cornering:	●●●○○○○○○○

FEATURES & COMMENTS
Rice-burner, crotch-rocket, call it what you want, this is one mean bike. Use it to nail any Unique Stunt Jump.

FREEWAY

Cool Factor:	●●●●●●●●○○
Speed:	●●●●○○○○○○
Handling:	●●●●●●○○○○
Cornering:	●●●●○○○○○○

FEATURES & COMMENTS
The Freeway is a cut above the Angel.

SANCHEZ

Cool Factor:	●●●●●●●○○○
Speed:	●●●●●●○○○○
Handling:	●●●●○○○○○○
Cornering:	●●●●●○○○○○

FEATURES & COMMENTS
Rides pretty well in the city, but really shows its stuff off-road!

ODD JOB VEHICLES

AMBULANCE

Cool Factor:	●●●●●○○○○○
Speed:	●●●●●○○○○○
Handling:	●●●●○○○○○○
Cornering:	●●●○○○○○○○

FEATURES & COMMENTS
Press the R3 Button to begin the Paramedic mission. Press the L3 Button (quickly) to trigger the siren. You can gain 20 health points from entering an Ambulance, but it won't put you over 100hp.

CABBIE

Cool Factor:	●●●○○○○○○○
Speed:	●●●○○○○○○○
Handling:	●●●○○○○○○○
Cornering:	●●○○○○○○○○

FEATURES & COMMENTS
Press R3 to begin Taxi Driver; however, this cab rolls over in the corners rather easily.

FBI RANCHER

Cool Factor:	●●●●●●●○○○
Speed:	●●●●●○○○○○
Handling:	●●●●●○○○○○
Cornering:	●●●●●○○○○○

FEATURES & COMMENTS
Press the R3 Button to trigger Vigilante mode. This vehicle handles very well for a vehicle of its size.

BARRACKS OL

Cool Factor:	●●●●●○○○○○
Speed:	●●●●●○○○○○
Handling:	●●●○○○○○○○
Cornering:	●●●○○○○○○○

FEATURES & COMMENTS
Press the R3 Button to trigger the Vigilante missions. This vehicle is great for crushing cars, but it will start to show its ugly side when reaching higher levels and faster vehicles.

ENFORCER

Cool Factor:	●●●●●●○○○○
Speed:	●●●●○○○○○○
Handling:	●●●●○○○○○○
Cornering:	●●●●○○○○○○

FEATURES & COMMENTS
Press the R3 Button to trigger the Vigilante missions. Whenever you exit an Enforcer, you emerge with full Body Armor (you'll probably need it).

FBI WASHINGTON

Cool Factor:	●●●●●○○○○○
Speed:	●●●●●●●○○○
Handling:	●●●●●○○○○○
Cornering:	●●●●●●○○○○

FEATURES & COMMENTS
Press the R3 Button to begin the Vigilante missions. The L3 Button starts and stops the siren.

FIRE TRUCK

Cool Factor:	●●●●●●●○○○
Speed:	●●●○○○○○○○
Handling:	●●●○○○○○○○
Cornering:	●●○○○○○○○○

FEATURES & COMMENTS

You can't participate in the Fire Truck missions without a Fire Truck. Press the R3 Button to begin and then L3 (quickly) to trigger the sirens. Use the Circle Button to turn on the forward hose and put out some fires.

KAUFMAN CAB

Cool Factor:	●●●○○○○○○○
Speed:	●●●●●○○○○○
Handling:	●●●●○○○○○○
Cornering:	●●○○○○○○○○

FEATURES & COMMENTS

Press the R3 Button to trigger "Taxi Driver." This cab is top-heavy and will roll over easily in the sharp turns.

PIZZA BOY

Cool Factor:	●○○○○○○○○○
Speed:	●●●○○○○○○○
Handling:	●●●○○○○○○○
Cornering:	●●●○○○○○○○

FEATURES & COMMENTS

Press the R3 Button to begin the Pizza Delivery missions. Use the Drive-by technique to throw pizzas in the direction of your customers, who are often found near Pizza restaurants.

PREDATOR

Cool Factor:	●●●●●○○○○○
Speed:	●●●●○○○○○○
Handling:	●●●○○○○○○○
Cornering:	●●○○○○○○○○

FEATURES & COMMENTS

Press the R3 Button for some Vigilante action on the high seas. Press the R1 Button to fire the cannons.

TAXI

Cool Factor:	●●●○○○○○○○
Speed:	●●●●●●○○○○
Handling:	●●●●●●○○○○
Cornering:	●●●●●○○○○○

FEATURES & COMMENTS

This is the best vehicle to use in the Taxi Driver missions. Press the R3 Button to start.

ULTIMATE VEHICLE

Cool Factor:	●●●●●●●●●○
Speed:	●●●●●●●●○○
Handling:	●●●●●●●●○○
Cornering:	●●●●●●●●○○

CONFIDENTIAL

FEATURES & COMMENTS

Once you've figured out how to get it (tip: the solution is hidden somewhere in this guide), press the R3 Button to begin the Vigilante mission 'Brown Thunder.'

MR. WHOOPEE

Cool Factor:	●●●●●●○○○○
Speed:	●●●○○○○○○○
Handling:	●●●●○○○○○○
Cornering:	●●●○○○○○○○

FEATURES & COMMENTS

Deliver a fix for the munchies! Press the L3 Button to begin the music and the Ice Cream deliveries (after purchasing the Cherry Popper Ice Cream factory).

POLICE

Cool Factor:	●●●●●●●○○○
Speed:	●●●●●●●○○○
Handling:	●●●●●●○○○○
Cornering:	●●●●●●○○○○

FEATURES & COMMENTS

Press the R3 Button to begin the Vigilante missions. Whenever you exit a police car, you emerge holding a shotgun with five shells!

RHINO

Cool Factor:	●●●●●●●●○○
Speed:	●●●○○○○○○○
Handling:	●●●●○○○○○○
Cornering:	●●●●●●○○○○

FEATURES & COMMENTS

Press the R3 Button to trigger the Vigilante missions, press the Circle Button to shoot, and use the Right Analog Stick to move your turret.

ZEBRA CAB

Cool Factor:	●●●●●●●○○○
Speed:	●●●●●●○○○○
Handling:	●●●●●○○○○○
Cornering:	●●●○○○○○○○

FEATURES & COMMENTS

Once you've unlocked this bad boy, your fares will never complain about how long it took you to reach their destination (press R3 for Taxi Driver).

RC VEHICLES

RC BANDIT

Cool Factor:	●	●	○	○	○	○	○	○	○	○
Speed:	●	●								
Handling:	●	●								
Cornering:	●	●	●	○						

FEATURES & COMMENTS
Find the correct Top Fun Van (Dirt Bike track) and crank up the action! Press the Circle Button to detonate, and use the Handbrake to get ahead of the pack in the turns.

RC RAIDER

Cool Factor:	●	●	●	○	○	○	○	○	○	○
Speed:	●	●								
Handling:	●	●								
Cornering:	●	●	●	●	●	○				

FEATURES & COMMENTS
Find this Top Fun van at the airport to begin the RC Raider challenge. The Raider is a blast, once you get past the large learning curve. Press the Circle Button to abort your flight.

RC BARON

Cool Factor:	●	●	●	○	○	○	○	○	○	○
Speed:	●	●	●	●	●	●	●			
Handling:	●	●	●	●	●					
Cornering:	●	●	○	○	○	○	○	○		

FEATURES & COMMENTS
Find the right Top Fun van (on the top floor of the large carpark next to the North Point Mall in Vice Point), then hop in and zip around the city from the front seat of a van.

SUVS & PICKUPS

BF INJECTION

Cool Factor:	●	●	●	●	●	●	●	●	○	○
Speed:	●	●	●	●	●	○				
Handling:	●	●	●	●	●	○				
Cornering:	●	●	●	●	●					

FEATURES & COMMENTS
There's a beach with dunes in Vice City!

LANDSTALKER

Cool Factor:	●	●	●	●	●	○	○	○	○	○
Speed:	●	●	●	●	●	○				
Handling:	●	●	●	●						
Cornering:	●	●	●	○						

FEATURES & COMMENTS
The Landstalker can carry the kids, dogs, groceries, as well as your arsenal of grenades and assault rifles.

PATRIOT

Cool Factor:	●	●	●	●	●	●	○	○	○	○
Speed:	●	●	●	●	●					
Handling:	●	●	●	●	●					
Cornering:	●	●	●	●	●					

FEATURES & COMMENTS
The Patriot is heavy, durable, and climbs like a billygoat.

BOBCAT

Cool Factor:	●	●	●	○	○	○	○	○	○	○
Speed:	●	●	●	●	●					
Handling:	●	●	●							
Cornering:	●	●	●	●	○	○	○	○		

FEATURES & COMMENTS
This truck is rugged and practical, with room in the back to carry a rowboat or your hunting dogs.

MESA GRANDE

Cool Factor:	●	●	●	●	●	●	●	○	○	○
Speed:	●	●	●	●	●	●				
Handling:	●	●	●	●	●	●				
Cornering:	●	●	●	●	●	○	○			

FEATURES & COMMENTS
This is much more than just your average jeep.

RANCHER

Cool Factor:	●	●	●	●	●	○	○	○	○	○
Speed:	●	●	●	●	●					
Handling:	●	●	●	●						
Cornering:	●	●	●	○	○	○	○	○		

FEATURES & COMMENTS
This is a great off-road vehicle. Find one by the Dirt Bike track to begin a 4x4 challenge.

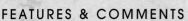

SANDKING

Cool Factor:	●	●	●	●	●	●	●	●	○	○
Speed:	●	●	●	●	○	○	○	○	○	○
Handling:	●	●	●	●	●	●	●	●	○	○
Cornering:	●	●	●	●	●	○	○	○	○	○

FEATURES & COMMENTS

The Sandking has great cornering for a tall SUV (tight suspension). Collect all the cars to fill garage 3 at the Showroom and this baby could be yours!

TRUCKS & BUSES

BENSON

Cool Factor:	●	●	○	○	○	○	○	○	○	○
Speed:	●	●	●	○	○	○	○	○	○	○
Handling:	●	●	●	○	○	○	○	○	○	○
Cornering:	●	●	●	○	○	○	○	○	○	○

FEATURES & COMMENTS

Good for blocking traffic—and moving furniture into all your new houses!

BUS

Cool Factor:	●	●	○	○	○	○	○	○	○	○
Speed:	●	●	●	○	○	○	○	○	○	○
Handling:	●	●	○	○	○	○	○	○	○	○
Cornering:	●	●	○	○	○	○	○	○	○	○

FEATURES & COMMENTS

Carries lots of people and still looks good—even if it's missing tires and rusting in a lot somewhere.

FLATBED

Cool Factor:	●	●	○	○	○	○	○	○	○	○
Speed:	●	●	●	●	○	○	○	○	○	○
Handling:	●	●	●	○	○	○	○	○	○	○
Cornering:	●	●	●	○	○	○	○	○	○	○

FEATURES & COMMENTS

Heavy-duty and durable, but slow.

MULE

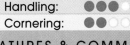

Cool Factor:	●	●	●	○	○	○	○	○	○	○
Speed:	●	●	●	○	○	○	○	○	○	○
Handling:	●	●	●	○	○	○	○	○	○	○
Cornering:	●	●	○	○	○	○	○	○	○	○

FEATURES & COMMENTS

Drives just like its name.

WALTON

Cool Factor:	●	●	●	○	○	○	○	○	○	○
Speed:	●	●	●	●	●	○	○	○	○	○
Handling:	●	●	●	●	●	○	○	○	○	○
Cornering:	●	●	●	●	○	○	○	○	○	○

FEATURES & COMMENTS

Goodnight, John Boy. Goodnight, Mary Ellen...

BOXVILLE

Cool Factor:	●	●	○	○	○	○	○	○	○	○
Speed:	●	●	●	○	○	○	○	○	○	○
Handling:	●	●	●	○	○	○	○	○	○	○
Cornering:	●	●	●	○	○	○	○	○	○	○

FEATURES & COMMENTS

This is just a commercial box truck—no frills.

COACH

Cool Factor:	●	●	●	○	○	○	○	○	○	○
Speed:	●	●	●	○	○	○	○	○	○	○
Handling:	●	●	○	○	○	○	○	○	○	○
Cornering:	●	○	○	○	○	○	○	○	○	○

FEATURES & COMMENTS

You'll love it if you're a drummer. You'll desire something else if you have any brain cells.

LINERUNNER

Cool Factor:	●	●	●	●	●	○	○	○	○	○
Speed:	●	●	●	●	●	○	○	○	○	○
Handling:	●	●	●	●	●	○	○	○	○	○
Cornering:	●	●	●	●	○	○	○	○	○	○

FEATURES & COMMENTS

It's big, heavy, and will clear anything in your path (but no chimp on board).

PACKER

Cool Factor:	●	●	●	○	○	○	○	○	○	○
Speed:	●	●	●	○	○	○	○	○	○	○
Handling:	●	●	●	●	○	○	○	○	○	○
Cornering:	●	●	○	○	○	○	○	○	○	○

FEATURES & COMMENTS

Not as fun to drive it as it is to speed up its ramp-like bed for some serious air!

SECURICAR

Cool Factor:	●●●●	
Speed:	●●●●	
Handling:	●●●●	
Cornering:	●●●	

FEATURES & COMMENTS
Very heavy and durable (almost bulletproof... almost).

SPAND EXPRESS

Cool Factor:	●●	
Speed:	●●●●	
Handling:	●●●●	
Cornering:	●●	

FEATURES & COMMENTS
Offers same day delivery.

TRASHMASTER

Cool Factor:	●●	
Speed:	●●●	
Handling:	●●●●	
Cornering:	●●●●	

FEATURES & COMMENTS
Cooler than driving a Perennial.

YANKEE

Cool Factor:	●●	
Speed:	●●●●	
Handling:	●●●●	
Cornering:	●●●	

FEATURES & COMMENTS
Moving? Call 1-800-Tommy-Vercetti!

VANS

BURRITO

Cool Factor:	●●●	
Speed:	●●●●	
Handling:	●●●●	
Cornering:	●●●	

FEATURES & COMMENTS
Not a bad ride for a van.

GANG BURRITO

Cool Factor:	●●●●	
Speed:	●●●●●	
Handling:	●●●●	
Cornering:	●●●	

FEATURES & COMMENTS
Burrito owned by gang members. Beware of the occupants when you jack one or else you will lose the van, your life, and the whole enchilada!

MOONBEAM

Cool Factor:	●●	
Speed:	●●●●	
Handling:	●●●	
Cornering:	●●●	

FEATURES & COMMENTS
Drive by and laugh at the losers driving the Perennial.

PONY

Cool Factor:	●●●	
Speed:	●●●●	
Handling:	●●●●	
Cornering:	●●●	

FEATURES & COMMENTS
No side or rear windows, double door in back, and no rear seats—great for skin-suit collecting.

RUMPO

Cool Factor:	●●	
Speed:	●●●●	
Handling:	●●	
Cornering:	●●	

FEATURES & COMMENTS
Pick up the girlfriend in this dream machine!

TOP FUN

Cool Factor:	●●●●	
Speed:	●●●●●●	
Handling:	●●●●●	
Cornering:	●●●●	

FEATURES & COMMENTS
Not so great for driving around, but when you find one, fun is just a step away.

Characters

TOMMY VERCETTI

Tommy's a 35 year old punk just out of the slammer, who served 15 years and is now back on the streets. He's connected with the Forelli family in Liberty City, and has been spotted in town with Ken Rosenberg at Escobar International. Something big is going down.

LANCE VANCE

Lance, a well-dressed 32-year-old transient, just recently arrived to Vice City with his brother who got popped during Sonny Forelli's drug deal—that went bad while under Tommy Vercetti's supervision. Now fighting alongside Tommy, Lance will stop at nothing to avenge his brother's death—no matter who steps up to the plate.

KEN ROSENBERG

A 33-year-old, high-strung lawyer, Ken has been trying to cultivate his relationship with his mob "friends" up North since 1978. Hence, he was overly enthusiastic to pick up their men at the airport for the big drug deal. Things went bad and now he has to save face with the Liberty City mob… or suffer the consequences.

THE COLONEL (JUAN GARCIA CORTEZ)

The retired Colonel, Juan Garcia Cortez, is an acquaintance of Ken Rosenberg. The Colonel helped Rosenberg set up the failed exchange that brought Tommy to Vice City. Cortez likes to throw extravagant parties on his huge yacht on the bay; Vice City's most influential citizens often attend his soirees, as does his beautiful daughter, Mercedes. These gatherings usually provide a chance to mingle with the local crime bosses.

AVERY CARRINGTON

Avery is the most one of the most influential and powerful criminals in Vice City. He's a 51-year old, strong willed southerner who's firmly rooted to his convictions. He serves up advice like it was universal holy truth.

RICARDO DIAZ

Ricardo Diaz, a.k.a. Mr. Coke, suffers from Napoleon-complex, which would explain his large gun collection. He bribed INS for a Green card in 1978 and is believed to be a major player in narcotics industry and. He gives to various *foundations* across Vice City, as well as Central and South America. Diaz has been mixed up in a long running battle for control of business in Vice City.

"BIG" MITCH BAKER

Baker is a Vietnam veteran, who was awarded the Purple Heart for obliterating an entire Vietcong village. He presently runs a local gang of bikers, but still harbors an acute animosity over the treatment of veterans. He's been jailed on 13 occasions, which were no doubt a result of his love for bar fights, eating live animals, wrestling, racing motorbikes, and urinating in public places.

STEVE SCOTT

A film director with an unnatural obsession with sharks and mountains of mashed potatoes, Steve Scott has been spotted at various parties with organized crime. Rumors say he's seeking any money he can get to finance his next big film.

UMBERTO ROBINA

This Cuban warlord can be found running his father's café in Little Havana. He's had a long-term feud with Haitian criminals, and wants control of their turf—even if it means a full-scale war. His bravery has been questioned within Cuban circles, mostly because he's never been personally implicated in a crime.

AUNTIE POULET

A larger than life elderly Haitian matriarch, Auntie Poulet is extremely dangerous if you're unfortunate enough to get on her bad side. She's believed to be involved in an age-old feud with Cuban crime families for control of eastern and downtown Vice City. She is heavily protected by Haitian thugs at all times.

PHIL CASSIDY

This redneck arms dealer is a member of several Vice City gun clubs and is believed to be involved in weapons trade. Cassidy claims to have served in various divisions of the U.S. Army, but military records show he was repeatedly rejected for service. Sources suggest he also distills "boomshine."

SONNY FORELLI

Sonny is the head of the Forelli Crime Family in Liberty City. He is believed to have major influence in racketeering, gambling, union trouble, corruption, and prostitution. Circumstantial evidence shows he ordered several mob killings, but only minor charges have ever stuck. Telephone records reveal calls to Ken Rosenberg.

Chapter 2

MAIN STORY MISSIONS

JUAN GARCIA

Introduction

The Forelli family sends Tommy Vercetti down south to take care of their new drug venture, and to keep him out of Liberty City. They need a man on the ground to do some work for them. Recently released from prison, set up with a little cash, and with the consent of the crime family, Tommy is unleashed in Vice City.

Naturally, things don't go as planned. Sent with some body-guards and a few suitcases of money, he is supposed to pick up a shipment of cocaine. The deal goes bad, and miracu-lously, Tommy, Lance, and Ken Rosenberg escape with their lives—but without the money.

This is where you take control. Return from the failed money exchange and visit the Ocean View Hotel to get some rest (and save your game).

Follow the pink blip on your map and park out front, then enter the hotel. Find the save tape near the check-in counter.

Once you're ready to begin the game proper, remain inside the hotel and walk into the blip near the stairs.

Side Missions

At this time, extra missions such as Taxi, Vigilante, Ambulance, Fire Fighter, Pizza Delivery, and any other challenges on this side of Vice City become available. It's a great idea to look around and begin your Hidden Packages hunt, as well—the rewards for finding these packages get better the more you find, making the big jobs easier.

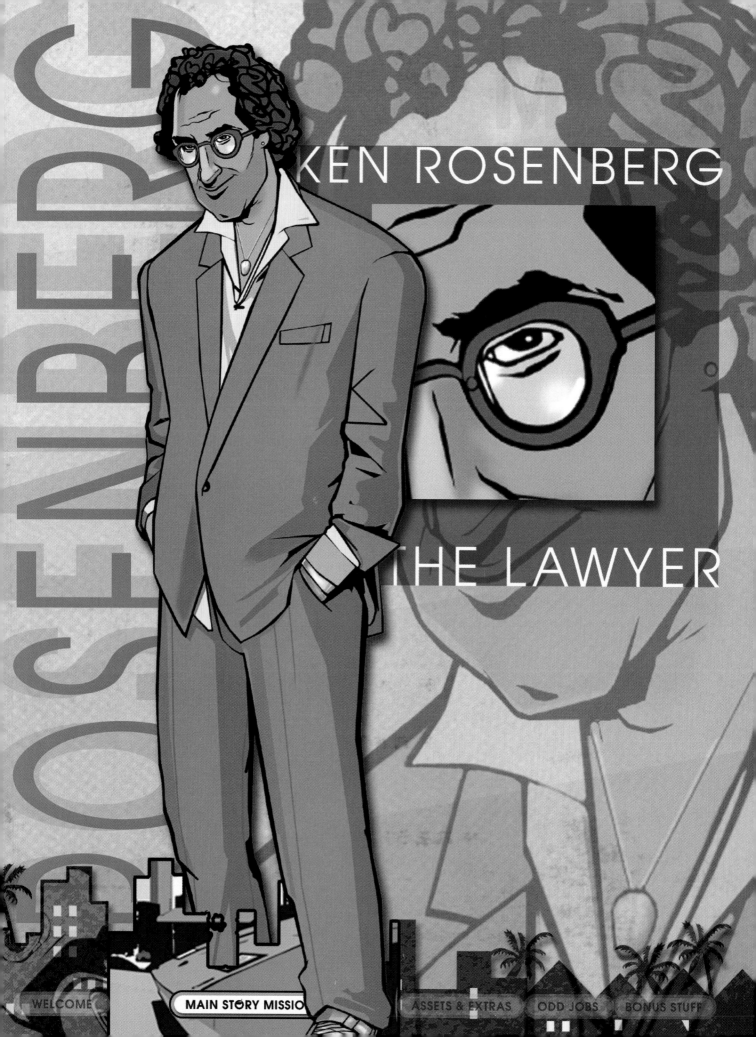

KEN ROSENBERG

THE LAWYER

Rosenberg

Rosenberg's Missions

AN OLD FRIEND

Sonny is upset that you lost his money. After swearing you'll get it back for him, you're off to visit the lawyer who set the deal in motion.

The lawyer, Ken Rosenberg, is a friend of the family. He provides your first few missions, and puts you in touch with some valuable contacts around the city.

Take this opportunity to drive around a bit (there's no time limit) and become familiar with the streets. The bridges over to the mainland are closed due to the Storm Warning, but there are plenty of other sights to see.

Find Rosenberg's office by following the **L** (Lawyer) on your radar, then enter his office to speak with him.

$ Payoff: N/A

? Description: Visit the lawyer, Ken Rosenberg, to get your first series of jobs.

BEACH **Rosenberg**

Ocean View Hotel

THE PARTY

Rosenberg tells you about a Colonel named Juan Garcia Cortez, who knows people around town. To meet with him, you need to attend one of his boat parties, and that involves getting a new set of clothes to look the part.

Follow the T-shirt icon on the radar to reach Rafael's, where you can pick up a snazzy new set of duds (that is to say, a funky '80s suit).

$ Payoff: $100

? Description: Put on your party clothes and check out the scene on the Colonel's boat.

Now, listen. He's holding his party out in the bay on his expensive yacht.

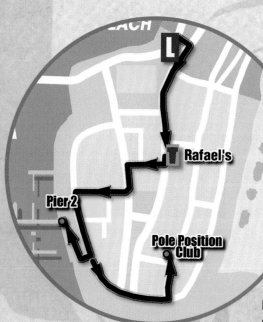

Once you have the clothes, someone will be foolish enough to leave an unguarded bike just outside the shop. Now you can cruise down to the Colonel's boat in style. Follow the blip on your radar to reach him, and enter the pink marker before the gate on the docks.

Once you board the boat, the Colonel apologizes for the incident, but this doesn't help you much—you still need to get the money and the coke back.

His daughter, Mercedes, befriends you and asks to be taken to the Pole Position Club.

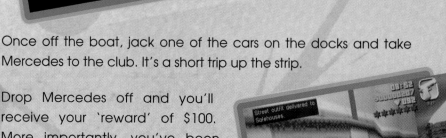

Properties

Notice the red house icon near the front door of the strip club. This symbolizes that the property can be purchased, but not at this time. After certain events occur, the house icon turns green and you may purchase the property, provided you have the funds. The property can then be used as a location to save your game and may include some extra benefits. See the Game Basics section of this guide for details on Properties and Asset Properties.

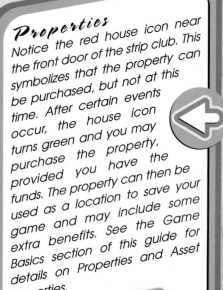

Once off the boat, jack one of the cars on the docks and take Mercedes to the club. It's a short trip up the strip.

Drop Mercedes off and you'll receive your 'reward' of $100. More importantly, you've been introduced to a new contact. Upon completion of this mission, the Soiree outfit becomes available whenever you enter the blip outside of Rafael's. The Street outfit is also delivered to all save houses.

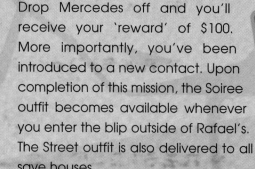

BACK ALLEY BRAWL

Rosenberg

Find Kent Paul, a music industry bigwig. Follow the blip to reach The Malibu, a local club. Inside, Kent suggests you check out a place on Ocean Drive. A Chef there could use a bit of knocking around for information.

Follow the green blip to reach his restaurant. He's hanging out in the back alley, and requires a little rough persuasion. Here's a chance to test out your physical skills (and see the new combo attacks in action).

Knocking him out gets you a cell phone... and a new ally. A strange man (Lance) shows up and starts talking to you. He throws you a piece to help with the escape from the dead Chef's posse. Follow Lance out to his car and hop in. A pack of angry chefs will be chasing you, but you can get away rather easily—if you haven't already taken care of them with Lance's weapon. But beware, shooting the chefs will alert the nearby cop walking his beat and place you at a Wanted Level 2.

Drive down the strip while following the Gun blip on the radar until you reach the local Ammu-Nation. After checking out the Ammu-Nation cinematic, remain in the car and return to your hotel. You'll get your reward for beating up the Chef, a meager $200.

- **Payoff:** $400
- **Description:** Issue a brutal brand of closing arguments to change some jurors' minds.

After the cell phone call, Rosenberg's pink marker reappears, making it possible to go in and talk to him again. There's trouble with Forelli's cousin, Giorgio—he's on trial and Rosenberg wants you to go rough up a pair of the jurors so they'll change their opinions. As you exit Ken's office, a Glendale misses you by inches, but careens into a guy in coveralls—making a Hammer appear over his body. Take the Hammer and enter the Glendale, then follow one of the two yellow blips on the radar that represent the two jurors you must intimidate.

BUNCH OF TOOLS

BEACH

L

Juror near the truck with the Hammers

You can head over to the Tool shop to pick up an instrument of persuasion (Hammer icon on the radar). But, you already have the hammer and that's all you need.

Assassination Missions

Your new cell phone rings after completing Back Alley Brawl. Answer it to receive a call intended for the man you stole the phone from—Leo. The man on the other end spills the beans about a buyer for Diaz's merchandise, and then becomes irate after discovering he's talking to a complete stranger.

Do not kill the Jurors or you will fail the mission. Just beat them into submission. Follow the yellow triangle blip to a hotel parking lot, north of the Malibu in Vice Point. The juror is nowhere to be found, but his Sentinel is pointed out. Use the Hammer to smash up all the car doors and the juror will exit the building. Seeing the madman smashing up his ride, he runs in fear—one down.

Knock! Knock!

Using Melee weapons on locked vehicle doors causes them to fall from their hinges, allowing you entry.

Follow the remaining yellow blip to the juror next to his car at an Ocean Beach restaurant. Hit him once and he dashes inside his vehicle. A truck carrying more hammers cuts him off in the street. Beat on the juror's door until it falls to the ground, then pull him out and beat him into submission. You can use a hammer to accomplish both tasks. When you're done, you'll be rewarded with $400. Sonny calls on the cell shortly after this mission to check on the status of his missing money.

RIOT

Rosenberg

Head to the lawyer's office again to speak to Rosenberg and his new acquaintance, Avery Carrington. Avery is a real estate king and enthusiastic Texan, and he becomes a useful ally in your escapades around town. Avery wants you to take care of some people who are reluctant to sell a property. To do this, you need to disguise yourself as a worker, and then go rough some of the real estate owners up.

First, head over to Rafael's to get fitted with the coveralls. Follow the blip to find your attire, then the regular blip to find the workers. Start a riot by getting in a fight with four workers. Keep moving to avoid taking too much damage.

Payoff: $1000

Description: Disguise yourself as a worker and rough up some of real estate owners.

New Contact

Another cell phone call directs you to the mall in Washington. It shows up on your map as a small phone icon. At this point, you can take the first Assassination mission (see page 87).

SPAND EXPRESS

N BEACH

PROTECT YOURSELF!

You may want to pick up some body armor and a weapon at Ammu-Nation (or from various locations indicated on the weapon map) before you go to the protest. With a pack of the workers chasing you, the security guards attacking, and the potential for a pretty high Wanted Level, this could be a dangerous mission.

Van Destruction Options

There are, of course, quite a few ways to accomplish the van destruction. You can drive them out and dispose of them, shoot them up directly, or use any other devious method you can come up with. It doesn't matter how you do it, just as long as the vans are destroyed.

Coveralls

The Coveralls that you were fitted with at Rafael's are now available at Tooled Up in the North Point Mall.

Avery Carrington

Upon completion of this mission, you can follow the **A** icon (Avery) on the radar. This leads to the Construction Site in Vice Point where you pick-up Avery Carrington's missions. However, let's proceed with the Colonel's missions first.

Once the riot is started, the security gate is opened and several of the guards come out to try to break it up.

You need to destroy the three vans inside the compound. Run in and beat up the security guard, then steal his gun and use it to detonate the barrels and destroy the vans. Drive the truck, parked by itself, over the security guard and up to the two other parked trucks. Shoot the red barrel from a safe distance to take out all three trucks in one shot. You can run behind the building if you need to escape the mob and gather yourself before you try this.

You'll get 1000 smackers for completing this mission, plus the satisfaction of knowing the first set of missions is complete.

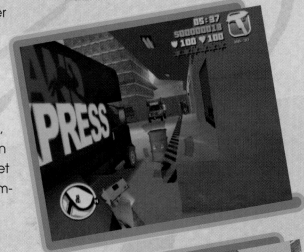

JUAN GARCIA CORTEZ

THE COLONEL

The Colonel's Missions

TREACHEROUS SWINE

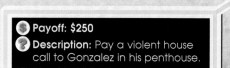

- **Payoff:** $250
- **Description:** Pay a violent house call to Gonzalez in his penthouse.

Time to Power-up

There's an Adrenaline behind Gonzalez's penthouse that could come in handy.

Casual Outfit

Upon successful completion of this mission, the Casual Outfit is delivered to the Gash in the North Point Mall.

The Colonel calls you on the cell phone and invites you to his boat once again. Follow the **C** icon on the radar to find it in the usual location. He has discovered the man who took your money. Gonzalez is your mark—or at least, so the Colonel says. Take the chainsaw and head toward his penthouse to dispose of him.

Follow the pink blip to the northern part of the island, and enter the building to find Gonzalez at the pool on the rooftop.

I'm going to shut that big mouth of yours!

Once you're up on the rooftop, take out his two guards and Gonzalez runs outside. Chase him and take him down. If you insist on using the chainsaw, deselect the weapon to catch up to him on foot, then punch him to knock him on the ground before selecting the weapon and letting him have it (holding the chainsaw while running slows you down).

Your Wanted Level immediately increases to 2 once he's dead, so you need to get to the Pay 'n' Spray in Vice Point, north of your location. If the car you arrived in is questionable, take a Cheetah from the hotel's parking lot, dodge the Police, then paint the car.

Once you're clean, the Colonel rewards you with $250.

MALL SHOOTOUT

The Colonel

The Colonel sends you up to the Washington Mall in Ocean Beach to meet a Courier. Since you are prompted to visit the Ammu-Nation, you can be certain you'll need some weaponry. Pick up a suit of Body Armor and an Ingram Mac 10, then head for Ocean Beach and the small vine-covered mall.

💲 Payoff: $500
❓ Description: Meet a Courier (and some surprises) in Ocean Beach.

Head inside and follow the yellow triangular blip on the radar up the escalator to the second level (triangles pointing up represent targets that are above Tommy's head). When you meet the Courier, a French SWAT team attacks and the Courier flees. Apparently, the Colonel is after something that the French military isn't particularly happy about him owning. You need to track the Courier down and recover the chips he's carrying before he gets away.

The violence that can hardly be avoided in the mall warrants a Wanted Level 2. Use the Adrenaline found behind the elevator on the first floor to aid in your escape.

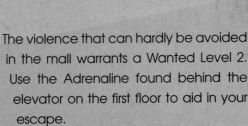

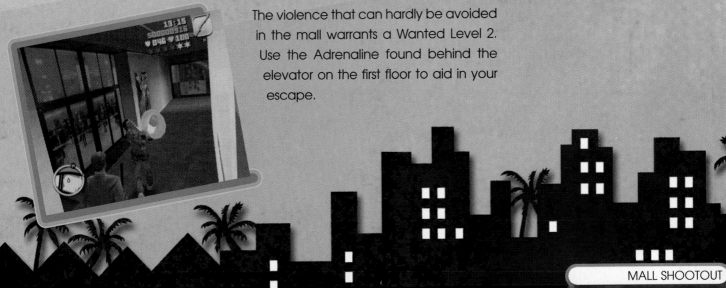

The Courier will likely escape the mall and find a car (or motorcycle) before you can catch up to him. Find a vehicle and chase him down, then wipe him out and retrieve the chips from the briefcase (blue blip). You must physically pick up the briefcase, so exit your vehicle (if you are in one) when he drops it.

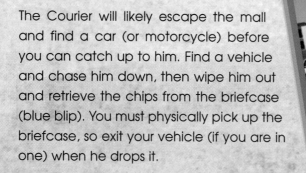

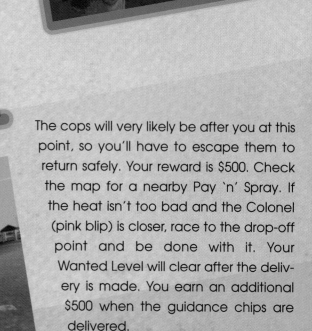

The cops will very likely be after you at this point, so you'll have to escape them to return safely. Your reward is $500. Check the map for a nearby Pay 'n' Spray. If the heat isn't too bad and the Colonel (pink blip) is closer, race to the drop-off point and be done with it. Your Wanted Level will clear after the delivery is made. You earn an additional $500 when the guidance chips are delivered.

GUARDIAN ANGELS

The Colonel

The Colonel wants you to grab a weapon and watch over Diaz and his men while a deal goes down. When you arrive at the weapon pick-up point (yellow triangle blip in the multistory carpark), Lance, the guy who showed up during Back Alley Brawl, appears and says he'll help you out. The two of you must guard Diaz and his men together.

$ Payoff: $1000

? Description: Guard Diaz and his men while a deal goes down.

Pick it up - then go and watch over Diaz's men at the drop off.

Look, you wanna do something other than just shadowing me everywhere? Why don't you come along and show me if you're any use.

Cone Crazy
Remember the location of this multistory carpark next to Rafael's. It's on the rooftop where you'll find the Stallion that triggers the Cone Crazy Odd Job later.

Protect Diaz
dirtbike

WASHINGTON BEACH

TLE
ANA

WASHINGTON B

Ruger & Lance inside the Carpark

They'll be here any minute - we both better get a good vantage point...

Drive Lance's car (or any vehicle in the garage) toward the pink blip. Once you arrive, Diaz tells you to get upstairs and wait. Enter the blip at the top of the stairs, then switch to first-person view with your new assault rifle (R1) and watch the alley below.

Several men show up and start talking to Diaz, but watch the street behind them. When the deal goes bad, unload on the Cubans who arrive in a pair of Voodoos in the alley, along with a couple vans from the street and the other side of the alley. It's best to remain at your vantage point for the duration of the gunfight—this helps prevent you from accidentally taking out Diaz yourself in all the confusion.

Watch for a third Voodoo to arrive from the street and keep an eye on Lance (the enemy may make it up to his vantage point). Once they're gone, a pair of Cubans on bikes show up and steal the money. When they try to make their getaway, Lance caps one of them in the head, causing him to fall from his bike.

MISSION REQUIREMENTS

If Diaz or Lance dies, or if you are too slow about saddling the Sanchez (dirt bike) and fail to follow the money closely, you will fail the mission.

Run across the street to grab the downed bike, then chase down the escaping money. Use the Circle Button to shoot straight ahead and fire at the escaping thief on his bike. Once you knock off the second biker, get the briefcase and return it to Diaz back in the shootout alley.

You'll get a reward, a cool $1000 in cash, ending the string of Colonel missions for now. This also opens Diaz's contact point at his mansion on Starfish Island.

RICARDO
DIAZ
COKE BARON

Diaz's Missions

THE CHASE

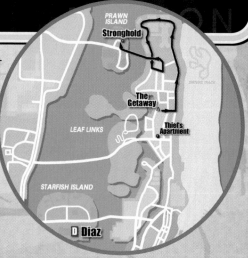

One of Diaz's dealers is skimming a bit off the top of the profits. He wants you to head to his apartment, then follow him to where he's stashing the cash.

Payoff: $1000

Description: Find out where one of Diaz's greedy dealers is hiding his unauthorized profits.

AVOID THE ROOFTOP HEAT
Be careful running over the rooftops. The man you're chasing will occasionally turn and fire at you, and when you reach an area with several explosive barrels, the shots ignite them. You can still safely jump through the flames to pursue him, though. If you're quick enough, this attack will never happen, so keep on him!

Follow the pink blip to reach the thief's apartment, then peek inside his window (indicated by the marker on the second floor). This spooks him and he runs for the rooftops. Chase after him over the buildings, jumping over the gaps or running across the planks that connect the rooftops, all the way to his getaway vehicle.

If you're really hurting, grab the Health icon from behind the dumpster. Take the Faggio, parked near the dumpster, or risk the Wanted Level and jack a faster vehicle that may be driving by. However, you must be quick to ensure the thief doesn't lose you. The escaping crook packs a Ruger and he'll merrily shoot up your ride, but you need him alive to find his hideout, so don't waste him.

Faggio Phenomena
Chasing the thief while on the Faggio, instead of a larger vehicle, makes you a smaller, more difficult target for the thief to shoot.

Continue the pursuit at a safe distance to avoid the Ruger bullets and he'll eventually lead you over to Prawn Island. Once you've caught up with him and discovered his stronghold, the mission is complete and you earn another $1000.

Diaz

Ricardo Diaz needs you to deal with the stronghold you discovered in the last mission. Lance shows up under the pseudonym of 'Quintin', and pilots a helicopter with you as the gunner.

> 💰 **Payoff:** $2000
> ❓ **Description:** Rattle the skimmer's Prawn Island stronghold with gun-fire from a helicopter.

He flies you to the grounds of the stronghold on Prawn Island with an M60 in hand. Unload and destroy all targets of opportunity from this lofty perch. Aim for any red explosive barrels you see—the explosion will do a lot of the work for you.

Don't take too long to eliminate the gunners on the various levels of the fortress, because the Helicopter's health is at stake. Keep an eye on the Heli Health below your Wanted Level and don't allow the enemy bullets to drain it. If the Helicopter is destroyed, your mission will fail.

Eliminating all the shooters in one area allows Lance to fly to the next. Once all areas are clear, Lance sets you down so you can enter the building. You will still be holding the M60, but now the ammo is limited. Be prepared for an ambush inside the stronghold. Run in, crouch to avoid fire, and take down the guards on both floors.

From there, head up the stairs, take out the guard at the door, then proceed to the rooftop and recover the cash in the brief-case. As soon as you get it, Lance will land, pick you up, take you back to the Mansion, and you'll be handsomely rewarded with $2000—plus, even more trust from Diaz.

Colonel Continued

Completing this mission opens the last of Colonel Cortez's missions and removes the roadblocks to the mainland. It's worth taking a quick break from the Diaz missions to complete the remaining jobs the Colonel has for you.

$ Payoff: $2000

? Description: Track down a mobile tank and steal it.

SIR, YES SIR!

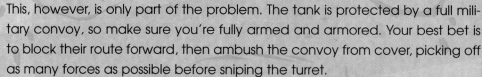

The Colonel wants you to retrieve a "piece of hardware." That is to say… a tank. Expect the military and the police to be less than pleased with you.

The tank is on the mainland, encompassing Downtown, Little Havana, and Little Haiti. Head across the bridge and follow the red blip to catch up with it.

This, however, is only part of the problem. The tank is protected by a full military convoy, so make sure you're fully armed and armored. Your best bet is to block their route forward, then ambush the convoy from cover, picking off as many forces as possible before sniping the turret.

Explosive Speed

Turn the tank's turret behind you and fire the cannon continually while driving forward. The result: small bursts of speed that help you beat the clock to the storage facility!

Once the turret is gone, run over to the driver's side door and bang on it with a melee weapon. The driver will escape, allowing you to commandeer the tank.

Park 'n' Go

If you park a car in front of the tank, the convoy will actually stop. Use this tactic to run over and beat the Rhino's door open with a Melee weapon, then hop right in the tank without dealing with the escort.

The military then activates the tank's self-destruct mechanism, and you are given a time limit to reach the Colonel's storage facility. Follow the pink blip to the garage and drop off the tank, fast!

You've earned another $2000. Now it's time for the last of the Colonel's missions.

ALL HANDS ON DECK

The Colonel has decided that getting out of town is in his best interest, and he wants you to help escort him to safety.

You'll be stuck on the deck of his yacht, assaulted from all sides, so be ready for some serious firefights. The French want their military guidance chips back, and they'll stop at nothing to get them.

$ Payoff: $5000

? Description: Escort the Colonel safely through a bevy of sea and air assaults.

DEFEND THE COLONEL

You can move from the upper to the lower deck. The first part of the mission involves dealing with several pursuing boats, so sink them from the vantage point of your choice. They'll appear on the starboard and port sides of the yacht.

CLEAR THE ROUTE

Next up is a cordon of ships blocking your path. Move up front and unload on them. When the helicopters' arrival is announced by a shipmate, head for the upper deck and destroy them (a Ruger and Health icon continually appear on the top deck as you run out of ammo and health). If you don't destroy both helicopters while they're in the air, the Frenchmen will board the ship and begin attacking. The helicopters will continue to pick up more men until they are destroyed.

GROUND THE APACHE

Your next target is a serious piece of military hardware—an Apache shows up and begins assaulting the boat, likely killing many of the guards on the upper deck. Keep a constant stream of bullets directed at the helicopter until it comes down. The regenerating assault rifle on the upper deck is excellent for this task.

CONTINUE CLEARING THE ROUTE

Once the Apache is gone, wipe out the ships blocking the Colonel's Yacht, if you haven't done so already. Use the first-person view with the Ruger (R1) to aim and shoot at the boats in the blockade. Once a path is cleared, the Colonel will happily sail away.

A massive $5000 is your reward for this big job, the last of the Colonel's missions. At this point in your career, it's probably time to think about acquiring some real estate. A few safe houses around town are a good place to start.

You should get a call from Kent Paul about now, but first you need to finish Diaz's last two missions before you can follow up on that lead.

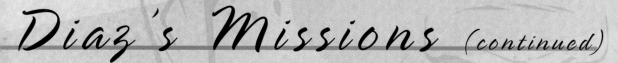

Diaz's Missions *(continued)*

THE FASTEST BOAT

- **Payoff: $4000**
- **Description:** Acquire the latest in boat technology in the Boatyard for Diaz.

Diaz is big on having a fast boat—and for good reason, from his perspective anyway. Rumor has it that a new boat is being developed down at the Boatyard, and he wants you to acquire it for him.

WASHINGTON BEACH

LITTLE HAVANA

Speed Boat

Follow the red blip to the big docks over on the mainland, far south in Viceport, then shoot your way through the riff-raff to get inside. You'll spot the boat, hoisted by a small crane. Walk inside the boathouse and into the marker near the crane controls to trigger the switch that lowers the boat. Exit the boathouse and fight your way through some thugs on your way to the lowered boat, then press the Triangle Button to enter the craft. Proceed to Diaz's mansion (pink blip on radar) on Starfish Island, avoiding the police boats and helicopter during the 3-star Wanted Level, and you'll earn another $4000.

SUPPLY & DEMAND

Diaz's final job is a bit tricky. There's a supplier who brings a boat loaded down with coke to Vice City once a month. The freelancer deals with the first boat to show up. Diaz wants you to take the new boat and get there before the other 'locals' do.

He sells his cargo to the first boat.

Payoff: $10,000

Description: Use Diaz's new high-tech boat to get his coke to the dealer first.

Head out to Diaz's dock behind the mansion and enter the pink marker. Once you reach the boat, you'll notice your new pal is waiting onboard. Lance shows up again to offer his assistance. You must race the other four boats to reach a sailboat first to complete the initial objective in this mission. You're commanding the boat, so you have no access to any weapons to ward off the competition. However, when you near the enemy boats, Lance will fire on them.

Let me guess, you thought I could use a guardian angel.

It's time for the Lance Vance Dance!

KEEP YOUR DISTANCE!

Be careful, the other boaters will take potshots at you if you get too close. You can drive-by shoot from the boat, but it's best (time-wise) to fly past them and just let Lance do the shooting.

Take the route to the left; the path that veers right is longer and requires you to navigate through lengthy, narrow channels. Once you have a comfortable lead, slow down and carefully navigate your way through the channel. If you're hasty and get caught up in the docks, the competition may get ahead and beat you to the supplier.

Tracksuit

Upon successful completion of this mission, the Tracksuit is delivered to Jockspot in Downtown.

When you reach the supplier, Lance takes control of the boat while you use the mounted heavy machine gun to wipe out the disgruntled losers chasing you. Immediately take aim at the shooter to quickly eliminate the main threat of damage to your boat. Next, aim for the driver if the boat is near yours (you don't need concussion damage). Finally, aim at the boat itself if it's far enough away. When Lance yells, shoot the gunners on the jetty before they dish out significant damage to your boat. Aim for the explosive barrels behind them to make this job easier.

Beyond the jetty-shooters, a helicopter whirls above with an armed thug hanging out the door taking potshots at you. Aim for the gunner and you'll either take him out or the helicopter depending on your aim—either will do.

Kent Paul Calls

After completing Supply & Demand, Kent Paul calls with an emergency. Something about Lance! Get to The Malibu ASAP!

There's one last boat ahead of you, past the jetty. Be careful about destroying it too close to your boat or the explosion that destroys it will leave you stranded. Your best bet is to get rid of the occupants and allow their boat to survive. After that, Lance returns you to Diaz's mansion.

This is the last time you'll work for Diaz, but it earns you $10,000.

Tommy

TOMMY VERCETTI

CRIMINAL EMPIRE

Tommy Vercetti's Missions

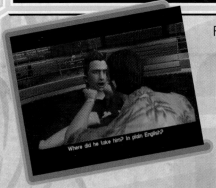

$ Payoff: No reward, but the goons at the Junkyard drop a lot of cash!

? Description: Rescue Lance from the junkyard so he can fight at your side another day.

Follow the **K** on the radar to The Malibu in Vice Point to meet with Kent Paul. Kent says Diaz has kidnapped Lance and imprisoned him in the junkyard. You need to rescue him. Swipe a fast ride and follow the green blip.

Get ready for a fight when you arrive at the alley leading to the junkyard in Little Haiti. Make sure you're well equipped before facing the numerous armed guards who are expecting trouble. They've also got a car blocking the entrance to the yard and gunmen surrounding it, but you can ram through this blockade without too much trouble. If your ride goes up, well, you can just take theirs.

Once you make it through the barricade, jump out of the car and eliminate any survivors to avoid fighting them later, after you rescue Lance—he must survive the trip back to the hospital or the mission will fail.

Take cover behind or under the machinery in the junkyard, then cut down all the guards in the area. Make sure you shoot the guy on top of the crane before entering the warehouse or he might kill Lance once the escape begins.

Tommy

You'll find Lance at the rear of the junkyard, just past the rock crusher in a garage. Dispatch the guards and evacuate the area with Lance. There's a weapon power-up behind the warehouse if you need more firepower, and the Sentinel parked next to the warehouse makes a great getaway car. If you don't take this car, one of Diaz's men might use it to follow you, so take it! As you leave the Junkyard, three car-loads of thugs in Comets try to prevent you from delivering Lance to the hospital. They have some heavy firepower and make good use of it!

LANCE IS LANGUISHING!

Lance's health gets worse as he is beaten, so you need to get him out of there before he expires. Avoid too much confrontation once out of the junkyard since Lance is in no condition to take on any heavy gun fighting.

Deliver Lance to the hospital (red blip on the radar) via the most direct route possible to avoid the hideously dangerous pursuers . Use the route mapped on the previous page to help you through this chaos. There's no cash reward for this mission, but tons of money is dropped at the junkyard—plus you get to keep Lance alive so he can fight alongside you another day. Tommy asks Lance to meet him at the Mansion on Starfish Island after he gets patched up at the hospital.

RUB OUT

The next mission is received from a pink marker just outside of Diaz's compound on Starfish Island. When you enter the marker, Lance drives up and displays his arsenal in the trunk (ala Pulp Fiction). The two of you must storm the mansion and eliminate Diaz.

$ Payoff: $50,000
? Description: Team up with Lance to rub out Diaz in his mansion.

GOT POWER-UPS?
If you think you need it, you can go all the way to the rooftop to find some Adrenaline tucked away in a corner and some health from the helipad.

Make sure you have a suit of armor before facing the trouble ahead. Use the (R1) first-person view while the M-16 is selected to shoot the two guards at the front door. This entrance is locked, so head around to the west side of the mansion. Proceed through a short hedge maze, taking out Diaz's men in the process, then enter the mansion proper.

Yeah, I like.

Protection Ring Missions
As soon as you have control over Diaz's mansion, a "V" for Vercetti appears on the radar over the mansion and a pink marker appears inside, at the entrance to the second floor office. Enter the marker to begin Tommy's own missions—jobs created by you and your friends to take control of Vice City.

Climb up the spiral stairs to reach the second floor (continuing up the stairs will put you on the helipad rooftop), then proceed down the hall to reach Diaz's inner sanctum.

Inside you'll be assaulted by several guards and Diaz himself. It won't take much to bring Diaz down. Doing so grants you the de facto ownership of his mansion, as well as a hefty $50,000 to start your own little criminal empire here in Vice City!

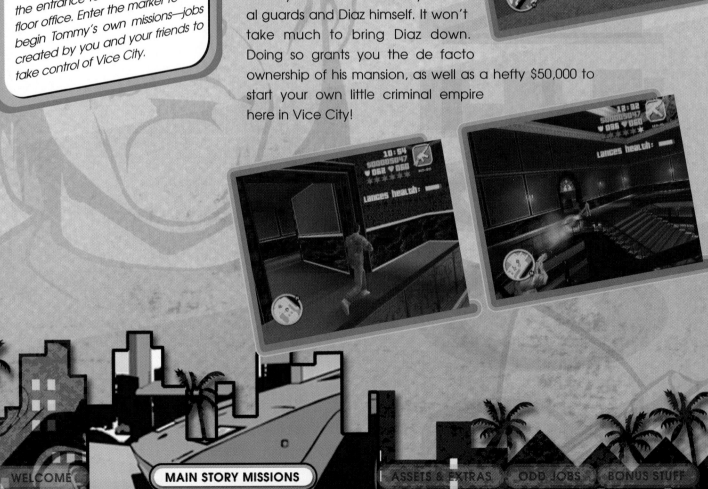

SHAKEDOWN

Tommy

PRAWN ISLAND

North Point Mall

DIRT TRACK

LEAF LINKS

STARFISH ISLAND

V Chez Tommy

$ Payoff: $2000

? Description: Pay a visit to some store owners at the North Point Mall that are reluctant to pay protection money. Convince them they need to comply by busting out their windows.

Now that Diaz is out of the picture and you own his mansion, you've got the power and the ambition to forge your own bonds of control over the city.

To get started, you need to scare the local businesses into paying protection money again. They're reluctant to do so, because they know Diaz is dead, so you need to persuade them.

You have only five minutes to make your case—you must reach North Point Mall in Vice Point as quickly as you can to conserve time on the clock.

Once inside, destroy all the windows belonging to the shops that refuse to pay. These shops appear as purple blips on the radar. You can use the grenades (available at the Ammu-Nation inside), as well as any rapid-fire weapons, to quickly bust and spray the windows. The purple triangle blips indicate storefronts on the top floor that require your attention.

Purchasable Assets
All Asset Properties become available for purchase upon completion of this mission. However, not all assets will generate daily cash immediately after purchase.

There are a few cops in the mall and a Wanted Level is almost unavoidable. Try not to aggravate the police. Run away from them and keep your focus on the storefronts. Make sure you break *every* pane of glass in each of the stores indicated on the radar as purple blips. If the cops are hot on your trail, enter the stores where the windows need smashing and the police will begin shooting through the glass to hit you! This will help speed things up. Finishing this job earns you another $2000. However, ruining the storefronts will also give you a Wanted Level 5, but even if you get Wasted or Busted on the way out, you still have finished the mission.

Love Fist Calling
After this mission (even if you fail), you should get a cell phone call, informing you that the Rock Band missions are available.

I'm saying is keep your eyes open and you might find the perfect business opportunity to catch Y'star.

MISSION PASSED! $2000

BAR BRAWL

Payoff: $4000

Description: Take out the thugs protecting the Front Page Bar and find out who supplied them.

Take your men to the Front Page Bar in Ocean Beach (indicated on your map with a yellow blip). You'll find a pair of security goons outside the bar, acting as protectors—these guys are infringing on your business. Take care of them (drive-by or run over them), then enter the pink marker at the top of the stairs near the sidewalk and the owner will tell you where the guards came from.

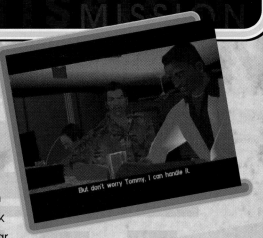

At this point, the clock starts to countdown from five minutes. If you do not finish off the rest of the targets within the time allotted, then the mission is failed. Follow the yellow blip created on your radar to reach the DBP security headquarters in Washington Beach. This is a good place to cause some mayhem and enforce your rule.

You can do this a few ways. Just rush in with your buddies supporting you; or, if you've got a few grenades handy, make the area hot for them. You can use the stairs in the alley across the street as a perch from which to snipe or throw bombs.

Once the guards in the parking lot are taken care of, two others flee on bikes (indicated by two yellow blips on the radar). If you have gained a Wanted Level from nearby cops on the beat, use the Police Bribe in the alley near the stairs to calm it down a bit. Quickly chase the two escaping guards down, ram them off their wheels, and finish them. You'll get $4000 for completing this mission.

Tommy

Enter the pink marker that appears on the front porch of the mansion. One of Tommy's men has screwed up a bomb job. You need to go and torch the place to cover up the foul-up, but to do that, you must be disguised as cops. Pick up a Wanted Level, and then let two cops follow you into the garage marked on your radar.

Payoff: $10,000 (+$10,000/day from Money icon on Mansion porch)

Description: Lure the cops to a garage in Vice Point, then detonate a bomb in the Tarbrush Café at North Point Mall.

Follow the pink blip on the radar to the garage in Vice Point. Try not to raise your Wanted Level until you reach the garage; this minimizes the likelihood of getting busted before you're ready to jump the cops.

Attract the attention of the cops and wait for more to show up near the garage. When the fuzz arrives, enter the garage and head toward the back, then run around to lure the cops to follow you. The garage door closes, and when it opens, you and Lance will be dressed in police uniforms.

Tommy and Lance emerge with their new duds, ready to penetrate the law's screen around the mall. Hop in the cruiser parked just outside the garage behind the short wall, then drive toward the police lines to the north (follow the pink blip to the North Point Mall).

Katana
Search the office behind the counter of the Tarbrush Café to find a Katana.

Enter the mall and proceed toward the pink blip to plant the new bomb inside the Tarbrush Café.

Enter the pink marker in the middle of the café to activate the bomb, and then quickly dash out. Avoid running too far ahead of Lance (yellow blip); you need him with you to complete the mission. The bomb detonates after five seconds, and when it does, your Wanted Level instantly rockets to five stars. Once you leave the mall, you'll need to hustle to reach the safe haven of your mansion.

You'll get $10,000 for completing this difficult mission. You may now also collect $10,000 per day from the Money icon on the front porch of your mansion. The Cop Outfit is also delivered to the Police Station in Washington Beach.

This mission is difficult, but you can slightly reduce the challenge by doing two things. First, park your getaway vehicle right out front, and be ready to get away as fast as possible. Second, plan your route home first, and check our map for a few nearby Police Bribes (see page 151) to lower your Wanted Level from a dangerous five to something more reasonable. Or, failing that, you can always rush all the way home, smashing through barricades and driving on flat tires!

At this point, you need to acquire at least 60% of the possible Assets in the game, as well as doing a few specific Extra missions to trigger the ending. Spend some time doing odd jobs, exploring the city, collecting packages, and generally enjoying yourself as a boss man. When you're ready, go on a buying spree, and be sure to purchase the Print Works and The Malibu to open up the last two Main Story missions.

Final Missions

CAP THE COLLECTOR

When you show up at the Print Works, you discover that the old man has been roughed up by the Forelli's—Sonny Forelli, specifically. They know about the little criminal empire you've established in Vice City, and they've come to collect.

Don't you worry, pop. I'm not angry with you.

Payoff: $30,000

Description: Knock off three pairs of collectors before they put you out of business.

There are pink blips on the map representing all of your asset properties. The one red blip indicates the first wave of tax collectors. There are six collectors in all (two on each Sanchez), but the reinforcements arrive only after capping the first two. They begin taxing the boathouse. You probably won't make it there in time to stop them from doing that, but you catch them as they leave. Hit the bike with a car, and then run them over as they attempt to get back on it.

Get Your Assets in Gear
Before you can access these final two missions, you must first complete several Property Asset missions. Skip ahead to page 68 for strategy on these jobs, then check out the mission tactics here to complete the Main Story.

Hanging out at one property and waiting for them to arrive is a bad idea; these guys are heavily armed and quick to tax. However, if you have a heavy weapon like a Rocket Launcher waiting for them, well… then that's a different story. The next target is Sunshine Autos. After that, they (or their replacements) will head for The Malibu. Continue to follow the red blip to track them down and play chicken with them. If they tax all of your properties, you fail the mission. Cap all six collectors before they do this and you win.

Finishing them all off earns you a nice $30,000—and it also unlocks the final mission!

The Mafia has arrived at the Car Showroom!

Payoff: $30,000

Description: Defend your mansion from a final onslaught of mobsters.

Enter the pink marker outside the front door of your Starfish Island mansion. Inside, you learn that the mob is coming, and they're not happy you killed their courier. Tommy sends Rosenberg to get some fake cash to pay off Sonny, and orders Lance to get the men.

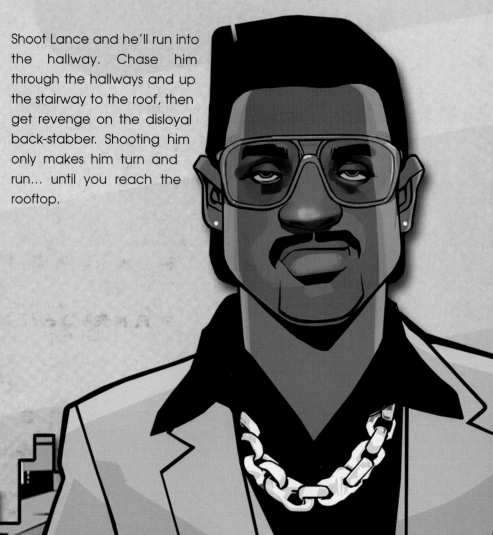

I just wanted to piss you off before I kill you.

Unfortunately, things don't turn out quite right. Lance has turned traitor, and he lets the mob know about your counterfeit operation. The mob pours in and assaults your mansion.

First, you've got to defend your safe. Protect it from the rush of goons. Shortly afterward (once you waste 15 goons or so), Lance shows up outside the office near the upstairs hallway.

Shoot Lance and he'll run into the hallway. Chase him through the hallways and up the stairway to the roof, then get revenge on the disloyal back-stabber. Shooting him only makes him turn and run... until you reach the rooftop.

Chair the Greeting Committee

Get a weapon you can aim with (there's a Python in the office's corner), then hang out behind your desk (or right around the corner inside the doorway) and blast thugs as they run up the stairs toward you. Standing at the doorway with an active flame-thrower works nicely, as well.

Robbery Warnings

You'll receive warnings that the mob is after your money, and cash will be deducted from your total if you don't stop them. If you have enough money, let 'em take it, just as long as there's enough for you to finish off Lance, then return to the thieves in the office.

Final Missions

Immediately run to the left corner of the roof and grab the Adrenaline to slow the action, then make a dash for the helipad and take the health. Hurry to the edge of the helipad overlooking the thugs and Lance, then take aim and pick them off one at a time (or shoot at the explosive barrels to kill several at once). Lance is tough—he'll take a lickin', but eventually stop tickin'. His weapon will also cause you some major hurt, so try to keep moving and crouching. Once you wax the traitor, quickly return to your safe; the mob will be going for it again. A Spaz Shotgun appears in the corner that used to hold the Colt Python.

Sonny comes in, Ruger in hand, with a whole host of backup. Quickly get back behind your desk again, and use it for cover while you take them out. You must eventually storm into the main room and take out Sonny—his back up will continually flow into the mansion. Survive this final, brutal attack wave and you'll own Vice City!

Oh, one other thing: The game doesn't really 'end' yet. You'll get another $30,000 and are free to play around in Vice City as much as you want now. and there's still plenty of business to be done. Congratulations... you've got counterfeit cash, lots of real estate, powerful friends, enough weaponry to start a small war, and plenty of fast cars to go wherever you want in style!

KEEP YOUR FRIENDS CLOSE

Chapter 3
ASSETS & EXTRAS

AVERY

CARRINGTON

Avery Carrington Missions

FOUR IRON

Avery sits and waits for you inside his limo at the construction site in Vice Point. He wants you to take care of some trouble for him on the local golf course. Guns are not permitted there, which makes it a good opportunity to take care of the target without his bodyguards interfering.

Hell, my daddy used to say, never look a gift horse in the mouth, and by golly, he never did.

Payoff: $500

Description: Hit the links and then practice your swing on one of Avery's targets.

Now head to the Leaf Links Golf Club.

Follow the blue T-shirt icon to get some golfing clothes, then head for the Leaf Links Golf Club (follow the pink blip on the radar). It's located just west of Vice Point, a bit southeast of Prawn Island. As you pass through security, all of your firearms will be checked at the door—you can collect them at the same location when you leave. Brass knuckles, swords, and knives will, however, make it past security.

You will find a golf club as you pass through security, but you will also receive one whenever you enter a Caddy, provided your Melee slot is empty. Follow the yellow blip until you find your mark's guards, then whack them with a golf club (or another weapon mentioned above), and he'll flee in a golf cart. Find your own golf cart and take off in, uh…hot pursuit.

His many guards will jump into Caddies and chase you around—some will even pursue on foot. Run over the guards on foot and continue to chase the target (yellow blip). If you take too long, he'll exit through the security check, find a car, and take to the streets. If he gets too far out of the way, you will fail the mission. Before hopping into a car to chase him, make sure to pick up your machine guns at the security check so you can perform drive-by shootings on his car.

The best strategy is to push past his guards on the driving platform and just start whacking him, regardless of his guards' attacks. Bring him down and Avery gives you $500.

DEMOLITION MAN MISSION

Avery asks you to get rid of an office building that's occupying some land he wants. Follow the pink blip to the Top Fun van located in Vice Point and jump in. The van is rigged with controls that enable you to fly an RC helicopter. You can use the helicopter to carry demolition charges over to the construction site.

- 💲 **Payoff:** $1000
- ❓ **Description:** Plant four explosive charges on the various floors of a building under construction. A seven-minute clock starts after you pick up the first explosive.

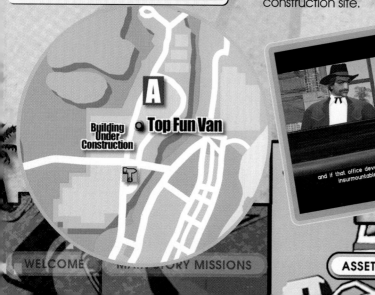

A — Top Fun Van

Building Under Construction

and if that office development were to face sudden and insurmountable structural problems, then I…

Follow the blips to the site across the street and plant all of the charges on the various floors of the building under construction. Of course, this wouldn't be fun without a time limit, right? After you plant the first explosive, you have seven minutes to place the remaining three.

Your best bet is to plant the explosives from the top floor down, giving you more time to complete the final drop-off.

Once you find the stairways that lead to the first interior floor, the next set of stairs is always adjacent to the flight that leads you to the floor you're on. The entire stair structure is set up in this fashion. After conquering stairway-navigation, the mission becomes a walk in the park.

RC Helicopter Controls

Press the X Button to increase speed and lift. Control direction with the Left Analog Stick. Press R2 for clockwise rotation and L2 for counterclockwise rotation. Press the Square Button to descend; press the R2 and L2 at the same time to look behind; and press the Circle Button to drop the bomb.

Watch out for the construction workers—they will gleefully chase down the RC helicopter and destroy it. A few security guards are posted, as well, and they carry firearms. Use its whirling blades as a makeshift sort of weapon.

Completing this mission earns you $1000.

Sonny Calls

After demolishing the building, Sonny, from Liberty City, calls to check up on your Vice City progress. This is just a social call; no harm or good comes from it...or does it?

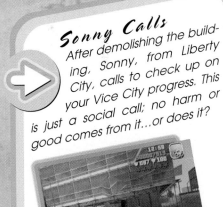

TWO BIT HIT

Payoff: $2500

Description: Start a gang war between the Cubans and Haitians.

Avery introduces you to Donald Love... remember him? (Well, your character obviously wouldn't be able to, but you just might.) He wants you to start a gang war between the Cubans and the Haitians (notice how Donald takes note of Avery's philosophy). Start by changing into a Cuban uniform. Head to Little Havana and follow the blue T-shirt blip on the radar to the clothing store.

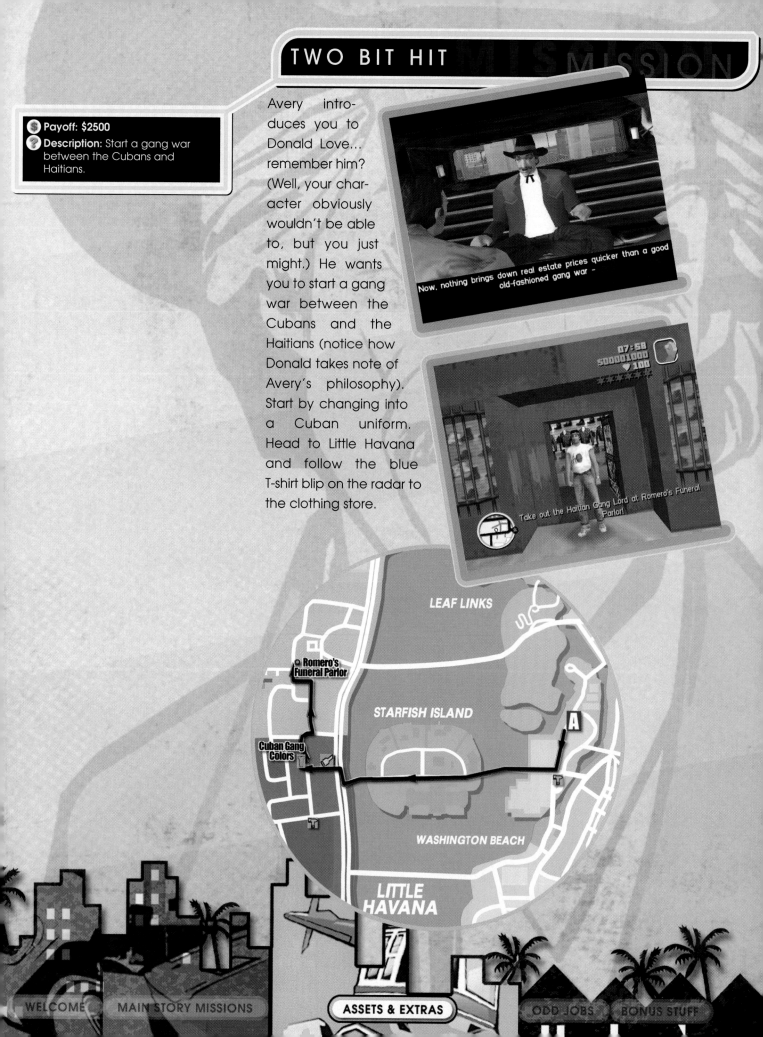

Now, nothing brings down real estate prices quicker than a good old-fashioned gang war ~

Take out the Haitian Gang Lord at Romero's Funeral Parlor!

LEAF LINKS

Romero's
Funeral Parlor

STARFISH ISLAND

A

Cuban Gang
Colors

WASHINGTON BEACH

LITTLE
HAVANA

Avery Carrington

Once you're in the right duds, go to Romero's Funeral Parlor and send the Haitian Gang Lord to an early grave (follow the yellow blip). When you drive by sporting the latest Cuban fashions, the Haitians will assume you're a member of their rival gang. This sparks the war that Avery is seeking.

The gang leader will very likely flee in a hearse if you don't waste him before he enters one. You can chase him down and use your drive-by shooting skills to destroy his vehicle. Be extra cautious when tailing the hearse—it will drop coffins that burst into fire when you run over them. Do not allow the hearse to get too far away, and switch vehicles if yours begins to burn after hitting a coffin mine. When the hearse is almost ready to explode, he will leap out and flee on foot. Pursue him using the drive-by technique or just run him over. After defeating the Haitian Gang Lord, leave Little Haiti to complete the mission.

Avery rewards you with $2500 for your services.

Cuban Call
Sometime after eliminating the Haitian Gang Lord, you'll get a call on the cell phone from Umberto, the Cuban leader, that unlocks the Cuban missions.

Havana Outfit
Upon successful completion of this mission, the Havana Outfit is delivered to Streetwear in Little Havana.

Rock Band Missions

LOVE JUICE

Follow the red circle icon on the radar to the Downtown V-Rock building to begin the Rock Band Missions. Love Fist want you to dig up some drugs for them—specifically, Love Juice. You'll have to track it down and acquire it for them.

💲 **Payoff:** $2000

❓ **Description:** Score some Love Juice for Love Fist.

You see, the thing is, Tom, the boys need some help.

Looking for something special? I got what you need!

Track the pink blip on the radar to find the dealer who carries the ingredients for Love Juice. Stop with a car (make sure it's a fast one) or a motorcycle, not on foot, and sound the horn while inside the pink marker. The dealer will approach, take your money, and then run. Chase after his PCJ 600 and mow him down, then exit your vehicle and pick up the briefcase of drugs (blue blip on the radar). The key is to use a PCJ 600 to shoot in front of you, or chase him in a very fast sports car; he's tough to catch on his PCJ 600 without one of these. Park in the pink marker facing the street so you can quickly take off after the dealer. If you get him off his bike alive, be aware that he is armed with a Stubby Shotgun.

After retrieving the goods, you'll get a call requesting some company for the band. Go to Mercedes' apartment in Vice Point to pick her up (following the pink blip on the radar).

Press the L1 button to pick up this weapon, it will replace any weapon you have of the same type.

Hey mate, the guys could do with some company, if you know what I mean...

Hiya, Tommy. And how are you?

After talking to Mercedes, you have one minute and thirty seconds to get her and the Love Juice back to the band before they take the stage. Follow the quickest route back to the V-Rock building (see our map on the previous page).

You receive $2000 for completing this mission.

Kent Paul Calls

Kent Paul calls on the cell phone after you deliver the Love Juice to the band. He says he needs biker security at the next gig. When the conversation ends, a pink marker appears at the studio, allowing you to speak to him in person. Just then, a major issue arises and the security idea is put on the backburner.

PSYCHO KILLER

Love Fist fear they've got a bit of a stalker problem, and they want you to take care of it.

$ Payoff: $4000

? Description: Take Love Fist's Psycho stalker off the fan list—for good!

Enter the the band limo parked outside the studio and drive to the area down the street where the band will be signing autographs. When the Psycho Killer pops a few fans and jumps into his car to flee the scene, follow him in the limo.

Rock Band

You need to eliminate him before he can cause any problems for Love Fist. A bright pink arrow appears above the Pyscho's car, but no marker appears on the radar, so don't lose sight of him or he may give you the slip! If he escapes, you fail the mission.

The toughest part of this job is catching up to him while driving the Love Fist limo; however, there is a trick you can try. Pick up the mission from the studio, then drive a fast car to the signing area. Run (or jack another car and drive) back to the studio and enter the Love Fist limo. Drive the limo into the pink marker at the signing, then immediately hop out. As soon as the Psycho goes nuts, jump into the fast car you have waiting, instead of using the limo! Chase the Psycho down, then ram his vehicle or drive-by shoot him. The key is getting into the waiting sports car quickly so you don't lose site of the Psycho's car. When he dies, the mission is a success and you earn $4000.

Biker Missions
You must complete the Biker missions before you can continue with the Love Fist jobs.

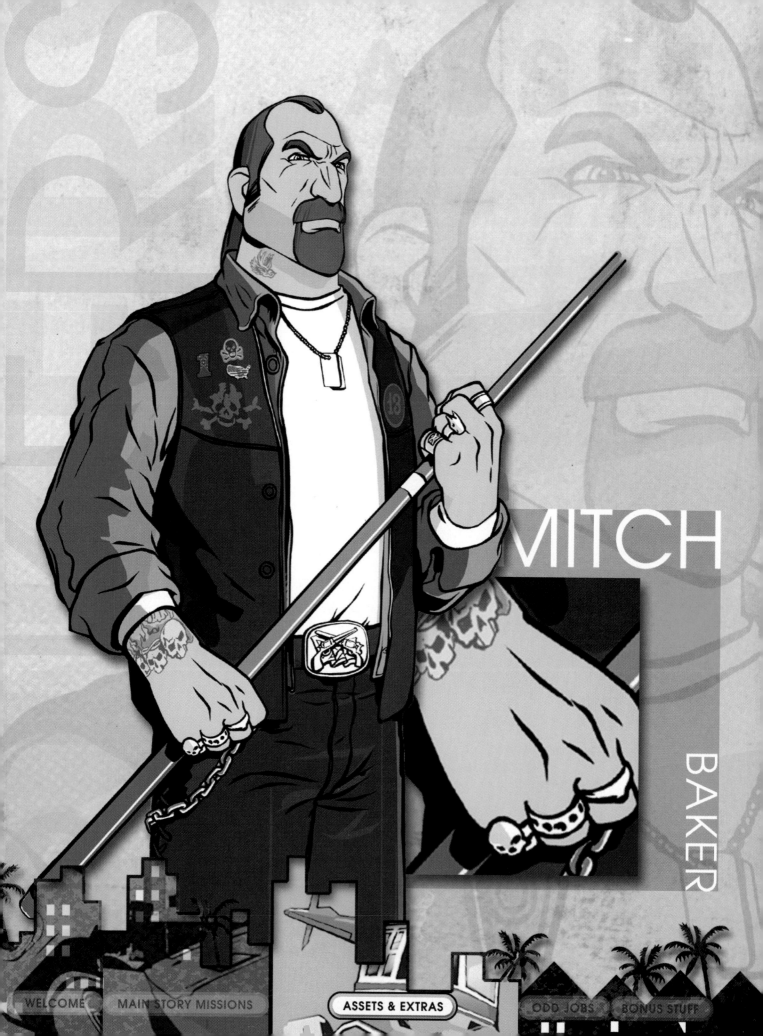

MITCH

BAKER

Biker Missions

ALLOY WHEELS OF STEEL

Head to the Downtown biker bar (Spade icon on the map) and walk into the pink marker just outside the door. Inside are the bikers that Kent Paul wants to use for security at one of Love Fist's gigs. Before the bikers agree to this proposition, Big Mitch wants you to prove you can ride by beating them in a race.

Payoff: $1000

Description: Race to victory against Big Mitch's gang to earn their respect.

This ain't no country club, boy. Can you handle a bike?

Go out and find either a Freeway or an Angel (motorcycles), and park it into the pink marker alongside the three other racing opponents outside the biker bar.

You can always find a couple of bikes parked outside the bar. Hop on one and begin the race.

Freeway vs. Angel

The bikes parked outside the bar are Angels. The Freeway is a faster, easier handling bike. Taking a little time to find a Freeway makes the race easier. To do this, jump on the Angel and drive around town; more bikes will appear on the streets if you're on a bike.

NO BUMPING, PEE-WEE

Do not attack the bikers or you will fail the mission. This means no shooting or hitting them before or after the race has begun. You can ram them with your bike during the race, but that's as violent as you can get.

an orial dium

DIRTBIKE TRACK

OWN

Checkpoint Race Route

Bikers ♠

Start

The race is a checkpoint affair, so drive carefully—it's much easier to spill from a bike than a car. Caution will win over speed. Once you have the lead, continue to drive safely and you'll be able to maintain that edge.

Win the race and you'll earn their respect, plus $1000.

MESSING WITH THE MAN

Payoff: $2000

Description: Max-out your Chaos Meter by raising hell around town.

Mitch wants you to show your biker spirit by raising some mayhem around town. This mission is structured a little differently than some of the others you've done so far.

Basically, you have two minutes to raise your Wanted Level, then increase your Chaos Meter to its max by destroying property, whacking passers by, and generally being a troublemaker.

Get your Wanted Level up to three or four to get a decent rate of increase for the Chaos Meter (the higher, the better), then drive around shooting and ramming anything you see. You'll hear a noise when you have successfully raised the meter. Using a bike for this challenge may not be safe. Find areas where you can cause chaos without the law easily getting at you, such as rooftops or behind half walls. When the Chaos Meter maxes out, the mission ends successfully and you're awarded $2000.

Pick a Safe Spot

Roughly, every four to five bullet hits to a car raises the Chaos Meter, and every four to five people wasted does the same. Using the M4 to open fire on cars and throwing Molotovs into crowds of people is the key to completing this mission in the time allotted.

HOG TIED

A local gang made the bad mistake of taking Mitch's bike. Mitch wants you to get it back for him, by any means necessary.

You get my bike back, you can tell Paul he's got his security.

$ Payoff: $4000

? Description: Reclaim Mitch's bike from the thieves atop Ammu-Nation.

The catch is, the bad guys are hiding up on top of the Ammu-Nation. You must make a stunt jump up there, then fight the thieves as they appear. Make sure to bring along some armor and a decent weapon, or you won't be able to stem the tide.

Grab an Angel, parked outside the biker bar, then follow the yellow marker to Ammu-Nation. Speed up the stairs of the building across from Ammu-Nation (as shown in the cutscene) to land on top of the building. While in the air, adjust your lean (forward and back) using the Left Analog Stick to ensure a soft landing.

Unique Stunt Bonus

The jump off the stairs to the Ammu-Nation is a Unique Stunt Jump! One down, 35 to go. (See our map on page 165 for the locations of all 36.)

Grab the Adrenaline from the rooftop, then begin shooting the enemies on the roof, as well as those that come running up from the stairs to the north. There's a health icon on the roof to help you survive the gunfight.

Head down the stairs and into the compound below. Follow the yellow blip on the radar to the garage containing Mitch's stolen Angel. Hop on the bike and continue shooting up the place.

Mitch Calls

After this mission, Mitch calls on the cell phone and agrees to work security for Love Fist. You can now complete the Love Fist missions.

Drive the bike to the west end of the compound and hang a right (north), then drive up the stairs and jump out onto the streets (near the taco restaurant).

Get moving! The heavily armed gang will give chase in Gang Burritos. They will shoot and ram with attempts to kill you or just destroy Mitch's bike, but either is very bad news. Return the bike to the bar and earn yourself another $4000. Now you can access Love Fist's final mission.

Rock Band Missions
(continued)

PUBLICITY TOUR

Love Fist need you as their personal chauffeur. Unfortunately, their personal limo has been rigged with a bomb that will detonate if you drive too slowly.

You need to keep the speed up long enough for the drummer to disarm the bomb. (Oddly enough, the drummer is the smartest member in this band.)

Be very careful around obstructions, as the Bomb Meter will increase quickly when you drive slowly, and ramming into a wall or car certainly qualifies as slow.

It takes the professor on the drum kit (Neil Peart humor) approximately 2 minutes and 20 seconds to defuse the bomb. It's best to head south and follow the road you're on to the east to reach the main strip that heads north and south down the coastline of the city. This is a long and wide street where you can easily avoid traffic. Once you reach the Chartered Libertine ship parked at the docks in Viceport, whip the car around to the opposite side of the street and head back the way you came. This gives you plenty of time for the drummer to defuse the bomb.

Just make sure to watch the Bomb Meter and don't drive so fast that you have to make another directional change on this street. Once the bomb is defused, take the band to the gig (follow the pink blip to the pink marker). Finish this mission to earn $8000.

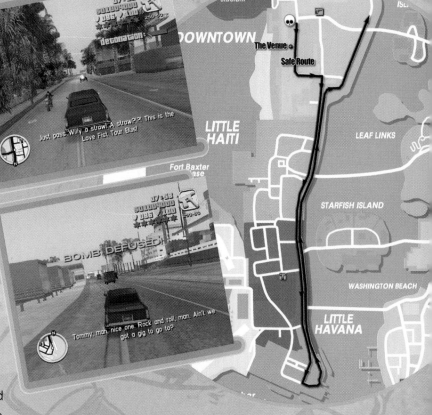

- **Payoff:** $8000
- **Description:** Safely drive the band around until the drummer disarms the bomb set to the limo's speedometer.

ASSASSINATION MISSIONS

Assassination Missions

Mystery Calls

Each of the Assassination missions is given at a different pay phone location around town. Just follow the current phone blip on your radar to reach the active phone. After completing each one, the mysterious caller will contact you on your cell and offer a new job. After the cell phone call, the pay phone icon will reappear on the radar and map.

ROAD KILL

Payoff: $500
Description: Plow down the Pizza Boy before he makes 50 deliveries.

Apparently, the cell phone you stole from the Chef was used to get Assassination jobs. Pay a visit to the phone icon location in Ocean Beach to receive your first job.

Mr. Teal, your help in eradicating those out-of-towners was invaluable to business.

The initial Assassination mission is relatively simple: Find Carl Pearson, a Pizza Deliveryman, and wax him.

The only thing is, you've got a time limit. He'll work toward making 50 deliveries, which will count down rapidly. However, he's on his Pizza Boy, so running him over is no problem. Track him down and grind him into the pavement to earn $500.

ON BEACH

Carl Pearson Pizza Delivery Man

Assassination

WASTE THE WIFE

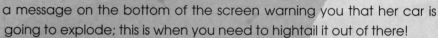

Payoff: $2000

Description: Usher Mrs. Dawson into a deadly "accident."

Answer the phone in Vice Point to take the second Assassination mission. Your next target is Mrs. Dawson. Your unnamed employer wants you to eliminate her, and make it look like a car accident.

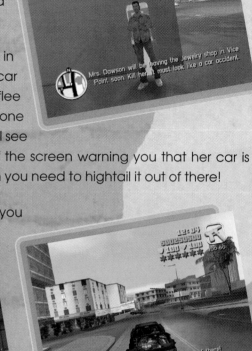

Find her leaving the jewelry store up in Vice Point. Follow her, and ram her car until it bursts into flames, then flee the area before it blows so no one links you to the accident. You'll see a message on the bottom of the screen warning you that her car is going to explode; this is when you need to hightail it out of there!

Successful completion earns you another $2000.

AUTOCIDE

Payoff: $4000

Description: Eliminate five gang members, scattered across town, to foil their intentions.

Take this job by answering the pay phone in Washington, near the mall. You learn that a European gang plans on hitting a bank convoy. Your employer and his associates do not want this to happen.

You need to eliminate all five gang members. A sniper rifle and submachine gun are provided for you (follow the blue blip to the backyard, west of the phone). Naturally, the catch is a time limit. Ten minutes seems generous, but you need to be quick about getting rid of your targets, or you'll burn up the time traveling from one place to the next. Follow your radar, drive fast, and you'll earn yourself $4000.

Your first target is Mark Griffon, who's working on an advertising board in Washington. He's literally up on the board, so your sniper rifle is the weapon of choice.

Dick Tanner is an employee of DBP Security on Ocean Drive. He spots your approach and runs. Chase him down and eliminate him if he manages to flee. Try driving up on him quickly to block his Securicar inside the yard where he's parked. As soon as you do this, lean out the window and begin shooting the grill of the Securicar full of submachine gun bullets. He'll push you out of the way, but you'll have already dealt enough damage that just a little more abuse on the road will do him in. Just as his vehicle is about to explode, he escapes and takes off running. Run him over or pop him drive-by style.

Part three of this killing spree targets both Marcus Hammond and Franco Carter, both of whom are located near the jewelry shop in Vice Point. As was the case with Tanner, these guys also flee if you are spotted upon approach. Find a vantage point from around a corner to snipe the tires from the truck—this makes the ensuing chase that much easier. One of the brothers always jumps out before the chase begins and tries to gun you down. Run him over, and then follow the truck. Ramming it takes too long, so use drive-by shootings to destroy his big vehicle. If you don't take him out quickly, he'll lead you too far from your next hit.

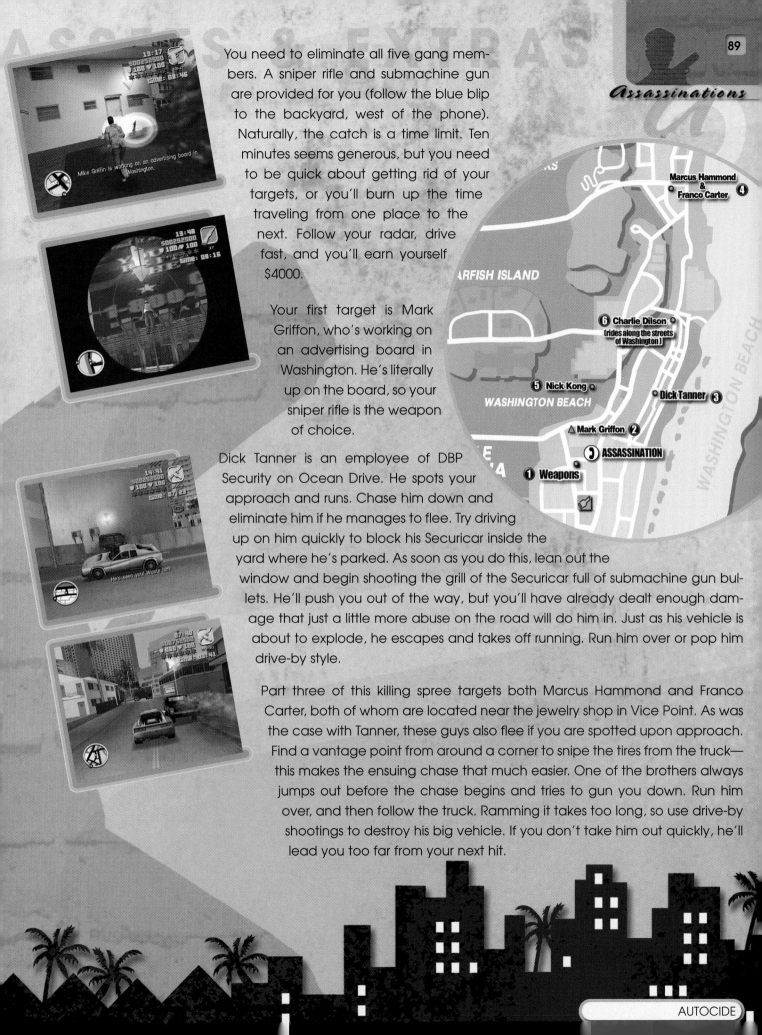

Nick Kong is down by Washington Beach, out in the water. No need to charter a boat, just stand on the coastline and snipe him without even getting your feet wet.

Charlie Dilson is riding around in Washington on a PCJ 600. Enough said... he won't last long up against any four-wheeled vehicle that you've chosen to chase him down in.

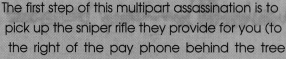

CHECK OUT AT THE CHECK-IN

This mission is accepted by answering the pay phone inside Escobar International Airport.

Payoff: $8000

Description: Snipe your target at the airport, then take his briefcase to the downtown Ammu-Nation.

The first step of this multipart assassination is to pick up the sniper rifle they provide for you (to the right of the pay phone behind the tree planter). Next, watch the woman on the balcony. Be careful when you're trailing her—she'll lead you close to the target and if you get too close to the man she speaks to, the Spook Meter will max out and you'll fail the mission. She'll approach your target and point him out to you. Snipe *him*, not her, then take the briefcase he drops. As soon as you pop him, you'll get tagged with a Wanted Level 2, plus the goons that you stole the case from will give chase (they want the briefcase just as much as you do).

Run out of the terminal through the cops and goons, then jack a fast car. Finally, carry the briefcase to the Ammu-Nation downtown. Naturally, the police will be hot on your tail. You can trek past either the Viceport or Little Haiti Pay 'n' Spray on your way to Ammu-Nation; just make sure you visit one of them. However, riding the Wanted Level will not lose the goons who shoot out of the sunroofs of the black Admirals. You will just have to outrun them.

Returning the briefcase earns you a hefty $8000 reward.

LOOSE ENDS

This mission is available after completing Malibu mission, "The Shootist."

Your mysterious employer instructs you to head to the top of the Cherry Popper Ice Cream Company. From this high perch, you'll find your targets and the merchandise he wants you to take to the heliport.

There is a gate to your left that leads to the back of the factory.

$ Payoff: $16,000

? Description: Snipe your way to the roof of the Cherry Popper Ice Cream building, acquire a briefcase, then return it via helicopter.

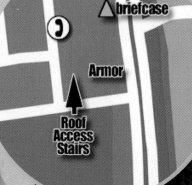

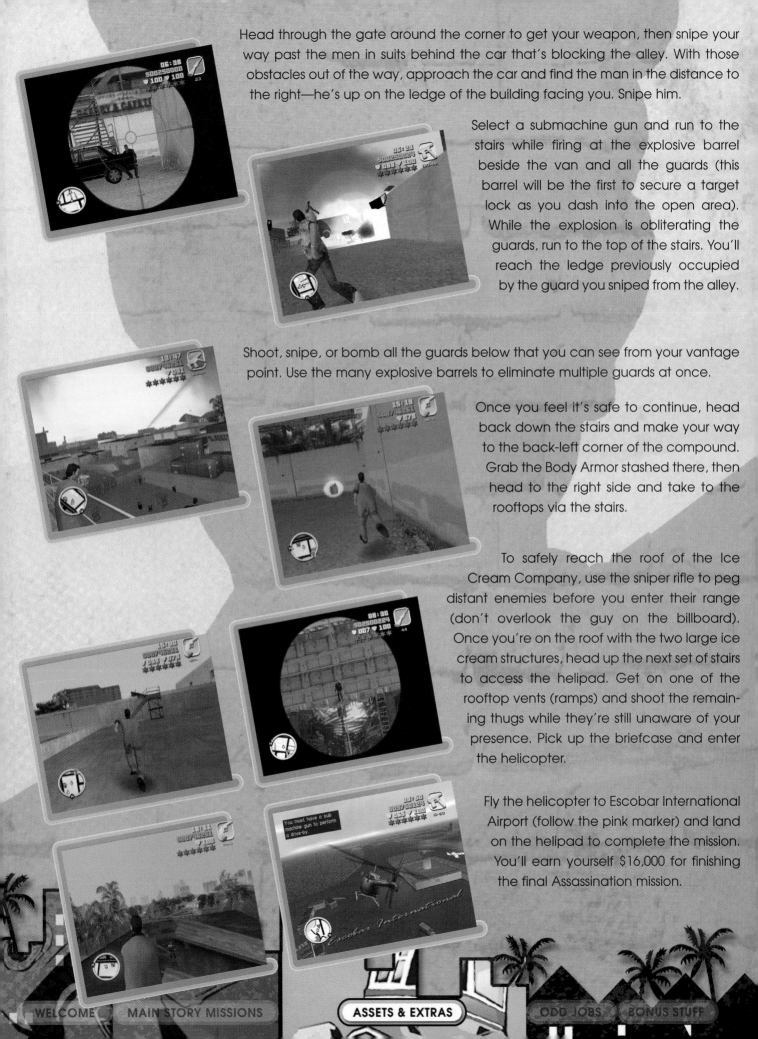

Head through the gate around the corner to get your weapon, then snipe your way past the men in suits behind the car that's blocking the alley. With those obstacles out of the way, approach the car and find the man in the distance to the right—he's up on the ledge of the building facing you. Snipe him.

Select a submachine gun and run to the stairs while firing at the explosive barrel beside the van and all the guards (this barrel will be the first to secure a target lock as you dash into the open area). While the explosion is obliterating the guards, run to the top of the stairs. You'll reach the ledge previously occupied by the guard you sniped from the alley.

Shoot, snipe, or bomb all the guards below that you can see from your vantage point. Use the many explosive barrels to eliminate multiple guards at once.

Once you feel it's safe to continue, head back down the stairs and make your way to the back-left corner of the compound. Grab the Body Armor stashed there, then head to the right side and take to the rooftops via the stairs.

To safely reach the roof of the Ice Cream Company, use the sniper rifle to peg distant enemies before you enter their range (don't overlook the guy on the billboard). Once you're on the roof with the two large ice cream structures, head up the next set of stairs to access the helipad. Get on one of the rooftop vents (ramps) and shoot the remaining thugs while they're still unaware of your presence. Pick up the briefcase and enter the helicopter.

Fly the helicopter to Escobar International Airport (follow the pink marker) and land on the helipad to complete the mission. You'll earn yourself $16,000 for finishing the final Assassination mission.

Porn Empire

3

STEVE SCOTT

Porn Empire

RECRUITMENT DRIVE

$ Payoff: $1000

? Description: Answer the casting call and find two sexy leading ladies for Tommy's film venture.

Tommy wants to make a bad film even "badder." He needs a couple of leading ladies. Your objective is to find Candy Suxxx and Mercedes, then bring them back to the film studio.

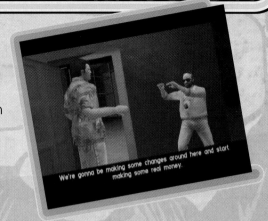

Follow the pink blip on the radar to the marker in Vice Point, then get out of your car and walk into the light. Candy's pimp pulls up in a car and unloads his armed passengers, then speeds off. Mow down the attacking thugs and take off after him (you can leave Candy where she is). Wiping out Candy's agent is somewhat easy. Continue the chase until he takes off on foot, then run him over and return to pick up Candy.

Take Candy with you and pick up Mercedes from the pizza joint (follow the green blip on the radar). Enter the pink marker inside the restaurant and Mercedes will agree to come with the both of you. Head back to the Studio with the girls, and lead them to Steve, the director. You earn $1000 and, notably, your name in the credits of their film!

(Map labels)
DIRTBIKE TRACK
Candy Suxxx
PRAWN ISLAND
Mercedes (inside pizza place)
Film Studio
LEAF LINKS

DILDO DODO

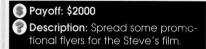

Run behind the studio and follow the red blip on the radar to the dock. Press the Triangle Button to enter the pontoon airplane parked in the water. Take off from the water, then turn north and head toward the Vice City mainland.

$ Payoff: $2000
? Description: Spread some promotional flyers for the Steve's film.

Get those flyers printed up?

Sonny Calls
Sometime after this mission, Sonny will call you on the cell phone to remind you that you're working for him. The plot thickens...

You can fly through the markers in any order, but the route is easiest if you start with the marker over the dirt bike trail Downtown. As soon as you pass through the marker, a nonstop flow of flyers spills out of the plane and down toward the city below. The propaganda begins. Turn south and continue to fly through each subsequent marker until you reach the last one. There are 12 markers to hit and a limited amount of fuel, so plan your route wisely.

Wyman Memorial Stadium

DOWNTOWN

LITTLE HAITI

Baxter base

Seaplane

LEAF LINKS

STARFISH ISLAND

WASHINGTON BEACH

LITTLE HAVANA

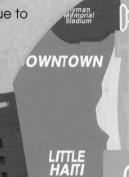

Follow the checkpoints around town, and when you're done, you'll earn $2000.

MARTHA'S MUG SHOT

- 💲 **Payoff:** $4000
- ❓ **Description:** Frame a meddling congressman by catching him red-handed with Candy Suxxx.

Congressman Alex Shrub is trying to get your type of film shut down. You need to frame him, using Candy as the bait.

Congressman Alex Shrub has jumped on the pre-election bandwagon, he's going after the puritan vote.

Steve gives you a camera as you leave the studio. Get in your car and allow the slow-strutting Candy to enter her limo outside the studio compound. Follow her in the helicopter to Alex's place in Vice Point. Enter the WK Chariot Hotel, across from the building Candy entered.

Map labels: Helicopter · DIRTBIKE TRACK · LEAF LINKS · Pay 'n' Spray · Alex Shrub's Party △ · △ WK Chariot Hotel

Find the side door to access the stairway to the top of the hotel. If you have difficulty finding the door to the interior hotel, then head to the beach (behind the hotel), find the stairs to the north side of the building, and follow the walkway to the door on your left. At the top of the stairs, select the camera and zoom in on Candy and the congressman on the rooftop of the building across the street. Snap three photos of the two of them together.

Head back to your studios with the incriminating pictures and a Wanted Level of five hanging over your head. Take advantage of a Pay 'n' Spray, or just try to gung-ho it and drive right back through the spike strips, helicopters, angry policemen, and FBI vehicles...Of course, if your helicopter is still in fine shape, hop in and fly back easily.

$4000 is your reward for finishing this mission—and you stay in business.

A Drive on the Beach

Escaping the police is much easier if you park your car on the sandy beach before entering the WK Chariot Hotel. Flee the hotel and hop into your waiting vehicle. Speed down the beach, heading north all the way to the North Point Mall, then race across the bridge to the studio.

Sonny Again!

After completing this mission, you receive a very disturbing call from Sonny. He's a little upset with you. He may turn into a threat that needs to be dealt with... soon!

G-SPOTLIGHT

Payoff: $8000
(plus $10,000/day studio money)

Description: Redirect a downtown spotlight to draw attention toward Tommy's star, Candy Suxxx.

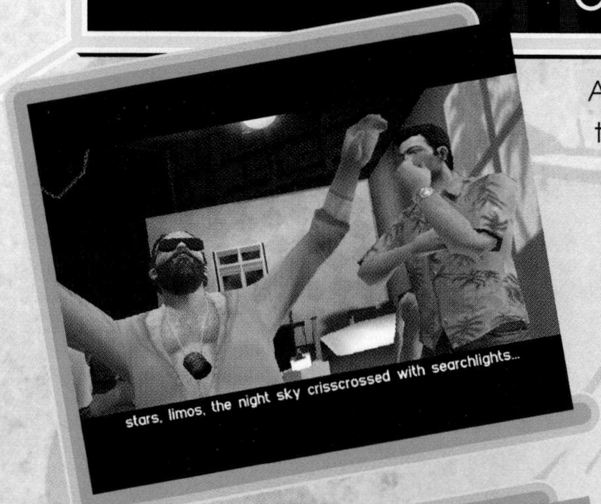

stars, limos, the night sky crisscrossed with searchlights...

As another promotional stunt for the launch of your videos, you need to head downtown and adjust the searchlight on top of an office building for a special light show.

INTER GLOBAL FILMS

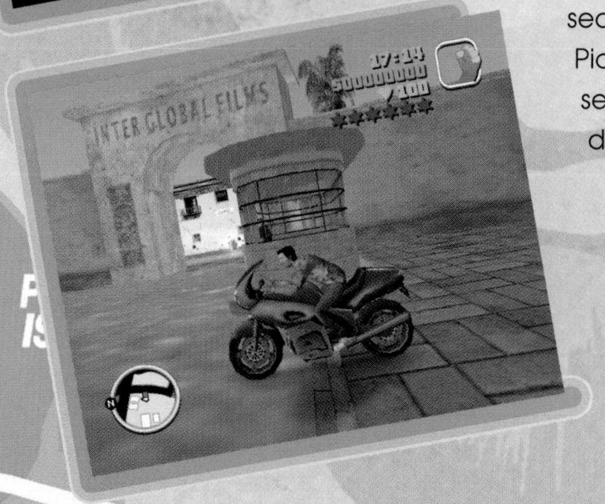

Of course, getting to the searchlight is a bit of a trick. Pick up the fast bike by the security guard station, then drive toward the blip.

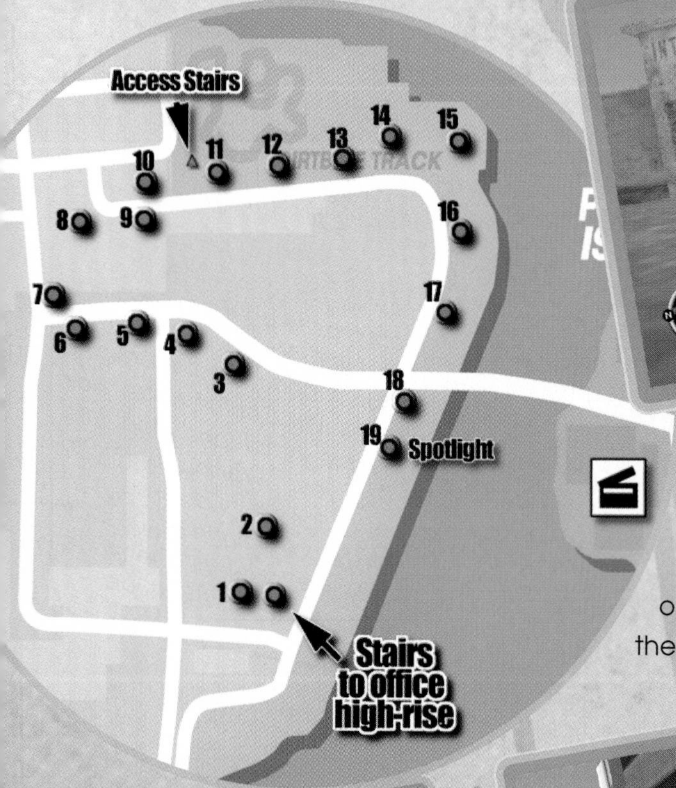

Access Stairs
1
2
3
4
5
6
7
8
9
10
11
12
13
14
15
16
17
18
19
Spotlight
Stairs to office high-rise

Once you're there, you'll see several blips that lead up through an office building, terminating in an open area where you must rev up, pop a wheelie, and go flying out into the open air to reach the next building.

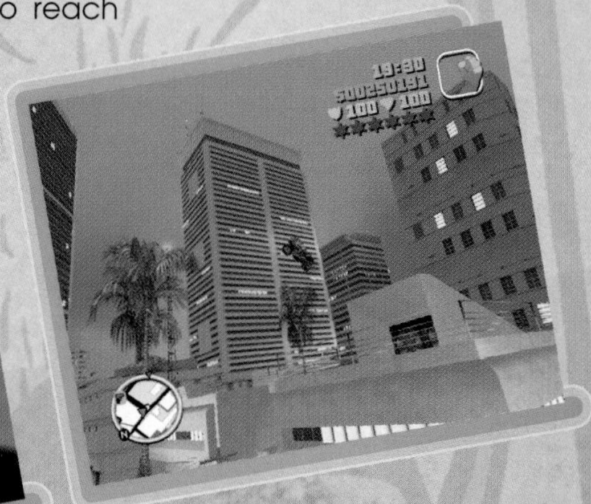

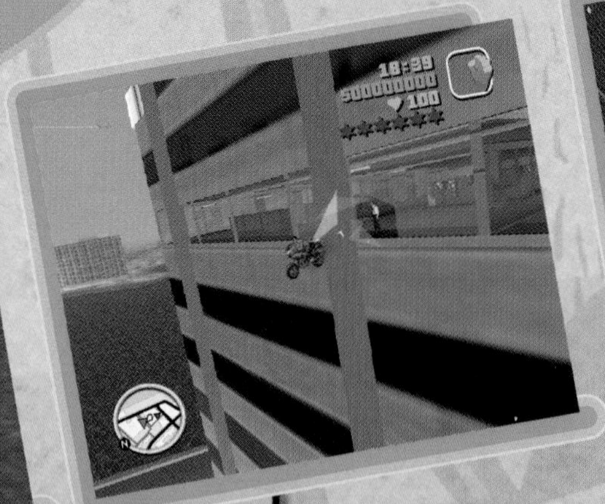

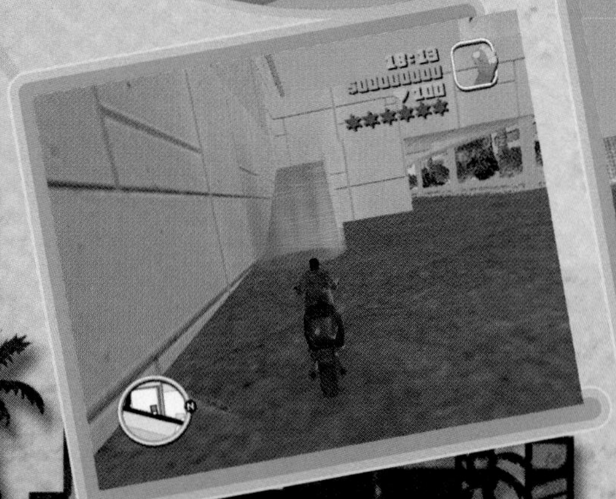

Continue to jump from building to building, following the pink blips. Take your time to find the longest strip of pavement so that you build up the necessary speed to make the bigger jumps. At one point, stairs lower on the side of a building, allowing you to return to the challenge halfway through instead of starting from the first building. Once you reach the spotlight, get off your bike and enter the pink marker. Tommy will cast the Candy Suxxx image on a side of a nearby building. That should get everyone's attention!

Completing this mission earns you a hefty $8000, and the film studio will now generate $10,000 a day!

UMBERTO

Cuban Missions

STUNT BOAT CHALLENGE

Pick up the Cuban missions by visiting Robina's Café in Little Havana. Stop in the quaint diner and speak with the Umberto. It's time to prove your worth in a boat race.

Payoff: $1000

Description: Navigate the Speeder through some watery checkpoints in less than three minutes.

Auntie Poulet

Auntie Poulet of the Haitians calls on the cell phone after you complete the stunt boat challenge. She invites you over to her house when you're ready for some interesting activities. The Haitian missions can begin now, but let's continue with the Cuban missions first.

Head out back and hop in the boat (Speeder), then proceed to the first checkpoint to start the challenge.

You've got three minutes to get through all the checkpoints. Follow the pink blips on your radar, hit the jumps at high speed, and be careful in the turns. The boat backs up very sluggishly, and you can lose a lot of time if you hit a wall and wind up in a corner.

Finishing the mission earns you some respect from the Cubans, along with a measly $1000 in cash.

Come on, drive for me again!

The Cubans want you to deliver a car, full of armed men, straight into the heart of the Haitians' territory.

Payoff: $2000

Description: Transport armed Cuban thugs into a Haitian stronghold and steal a van full of drugs.

Van
park here with Cuban gang
Sniper

STARFI

return the van here

park 4-door here

Umberto

07:09
$00500000
073 100

Sniper on the roof!

Get a four-door car, pick up the Cubans from Robina's Café, then head for the pink blip on your radar to drop them off. Be careful, the Haitians will be gunning for you.

Once you arrive, hop out and give the Cubans some fire support. The first group to attack is located at the end of an alley hidden behind a parked car.

There are a number of ways to get through the barricade. You can just shoot up the car and allow it to explode, decimating all the men behind it. An alternative method is to rig a car with a bomb from 8-ball's, race it down the alley toward the barricade, bail out of the car at a safe distance, and then detonate the vehicle when it reaches the parked car. Other options include sniping all the Cubans behind the car, firing a shell from the Rocket Launcher (check our map on page 151 for weapon locations), or tossing Grenades or Molotovs their way.

After you wipe out the initial pack of Haitians, a sniper on the roof pins down your men. You need to get up ahead to clear a path for the reinforcements. Take the PSG-1 near the concrete wall at the entrance to the compound. However, you don't really need a scope to nail the sniper—just aim any weapon that enters first-person-aiming view and shoot below the pink arrow that points toward the man on the roof.

Once you penetrate the complex, you must steal the van loaded with drugs and drive it to the restaurant. Avoid destroying the van in the gun battle or on your way to the drop off. You can also fail the mission if you waste too many of your own men at any time during this mission. Once the van is back at Robina's Café, the mission is complete and you earn $2000.

NAVAL ENGAGEMENT

Umberto is angry with the Haitians again, and he wants you to intercept a shipment out on the waters. Drive toward the pink blip to meet with Rico on the dock in Viceport. He'll take you to the shipment location and hand you a Ruger. The Ruger has a small amount of ammo, so if you are partial to this weapon, you may want to bring your own to add to the ammo.

💲 **Payoff: $4000**
❓ **Description:** Gun down some Haitians from your boat, then retrieve a pair of briefcases filled with drugs.

You assume the role of the gunner in this mission, and you're targeting Haitians with the goods you must recover for Umberto. Use any weapon with good aiming capabilities, preferably the sniper rifle. Once the occupants of the boats have been released from their soul cages, Rico can pull up to the dock and let you out. It takes practice to nail all the assailants in time before they destroy Rico's boat—and you don't want to be stranded out in the water with a burning boat. If you bring a Rocket Launcher with you, taking the boats out of commission is a lot easier.

STARFISH
Take out the enemy and grab the two briefcases

Jack a car and get back to Umberto's

Umberto

WASHINGTON BE

LITTLE HAVANA

Rico

Hop on shore and follow the purple blips to retrieve the two briefcases filled with drugs. One is near the vessels around the boathouse, while the other is heavily guarded near the house. Shoot the place up, take the goods, and return them to Umberto at Robina's Café for $4000. Rico's boat is annihilated as soon as you pick up the second briefcase. There's no need to take to the water again—just jack a car and drive there.

A Wanted Level of 3 is likely, and police patrol the water and the roads. The Wanted Level will grow to a Level 5, so you stand a better chance on land. Find Police Bribes or a nearby Pay 'n' Spray to shake the heat.

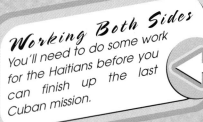

Working Both Sides
You'll need to do some work for the Haitians before you can finish up the last Cuban mission.

POULET

AUNTIE

Haitian Missions

JUJU SCRAMBLE

Visit Auntie Poulet's house in Little Haiti and share some special brew with her. That stuff will make you putty in her hands! She wants you to retrieve several stashes before the cops pick them up.

Hop in a vehicle and follow the yellow blip to reach the first powder pick-up location. Park your car close to the steps of the building near the junkyard so you can quickly enter your vehicle when you run from the bullets after the pick-up.

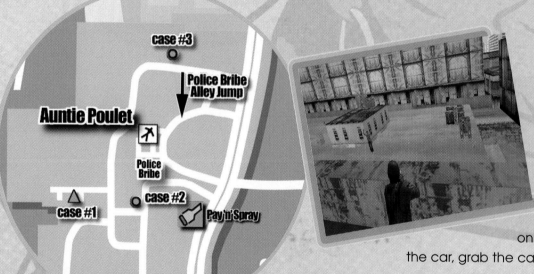

When you pick up the first one from the rooftop, you'll get a Wanted Level 2. This makes getting to the next one intact within a minute even tougher. Run past the SWAT gunner on the rooftop and enter your car parked below. Race to the second package location on a nearby corner. Jump out of the car, grab the case, and hustle back in.

Again, your Wanted Level increases, this time to four—and yes, you must acquire another package within a minute. There's no time for Pay 'n' Spray, so locate the closest Police Bribe to lower the Wanted Level. Just one bribe makes it that much easier on you.

Follow the final yellow blip on the radar to the small lot between two buildings. Drive your vehicle right up to the package to avoid flying bullets until the last minute before exiting to retrieve the briefcase. Re-enter the vehicle and drive straight across the street, into the alley, over the ramp, and through another Police Bribe. The last package raises your Wanted Level to five stars. Survive this intense pursuit and return to Auntie Poulet's in one piece to finish the mission and earn a whopping $1000.

Foil the Fuzz
There's a nearby Pay 'n' Spray, so take advantage of it—five stars is a lot to deal with, and you don't have a time limit for the return.

BOMBS AWAY!

Payoff: $2000

Description: Eliminate some Cubans and their boats with an RC plane that drops explosives.

Auntie Poulet is working her magic on Tommy again, and this time, she's using you to wipe out the Cuban boats.

RC Bi-plane Controls

Do not let go of the X Button (Gas) when flying an RC Bi-plane or it will dive, and recovery is difficult. Since the bomb you're carrying is heavy, you must pull down on the Analog Stick to lift the nose up and maintain an even altitude. The Triangle Button cancels the flight altogether and uses one of the three planes given to you during the mission. The Square Button drops bombs, which are unlimited per plane.

Drive toward the yellow blip on the radar to locate the Top Fun van. You're going to use an RC Plane with some explosives to destroy the boats.

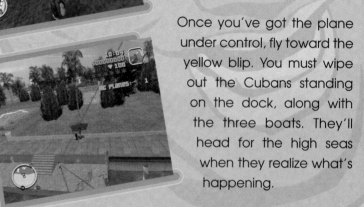

Once you've got the plane under control, fly toward the yellow blip. You must wipe out the Cubans standing on the dock, along with the three boats. They'll head for the high seas when they realize what's happening.

Dive Bombing

Destroying the boats is the hardest part of this mission. Try Kamikaze with your first plane while all three boats are parked at the dock. One explosion can take out all three boats when they're that close. If you chase them around, it helps to fly behind them, while matching their speed and direction. Once you're lined up, dive down and drop the bombs on top of them. Increase your altitude once a bomb is released to avoid the enemies' attack.

Destroy all three boats, then deal with the Cuban trying to get away in the vehicle—and make sure there aren't any others walking around (look for the green blips on the radar). Once you've cleaned up, you'll finish the mission and earn $2000.

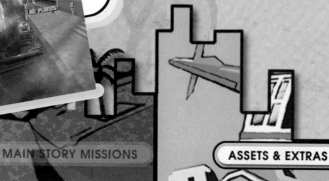

DIRTY LICKIN'S

Haitians

There's a major conflict between the Cubans and the Haitians brewing.

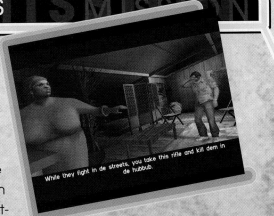

While they fight in de streets, you take this rifle and kill dem in de hubbub.

💲 **Payoff:** $4000
❓ **Description:** Snipe the Cubans from the top of a building before they beat the Haitians into oblivion.

Auntie Poulet wants you to give the Cubans a nasty surprise in the form of a sniper rifle. You can't be spotted, though, so find a vantage point out of the way and start picking off as many Cubans as possible.

Once outside of Auntie Poulet's, hike it over to the southeast street corner and you'll see a mob of people near the highway with arrows over their heads. These are your targets. To the north of the brawl is a building with a set of stairs in the back. Grab the Adrenaline icon from under the stairs to slow the clock, and then climb the stairs.

pick up Adrenaline
vantage point
Cuban Targets

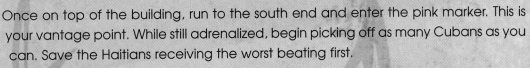

Once on top of the building, run to the south end and enter the pink marker. This is your vantage point. While still adrenalized, begin picking off as many Cubans as you can. Save the Haitians receiving the worst beating first.

Substantial reinforcements arrive for the Cubans, so stay the course, and continue sniping as quickly and accurately as you can. Avoid shooting the Haitians (Blue Shirts). You don't need to help the enemy, and if all the Haitians die, the mission will fail.

If the Haitians survive and win the fight, you'll finish the mission and earn $4000, plus you can go back to Robina's Café to finish the final Cuban mission.

Cuban Missions (continued)

TROJAN VOODOO

Then you go around to the Haitians processing plant, and you use their solvent as an explosive.

Payoff: $10,000

Description: Steal a Voodoo in Little Haiti to infiltrate the Haitian compound, then blow the joint sky high by planting some bombs in the factory.

Umberto wants you to go with Pepe to Little Haiti and steal a Voodoo car. This task is easy enough since you know there's always one parked in front of Auntie Poulet's house.

bomb locations inside Drug Factory

Rico

Voodoo Location

park in pink marker in the Drug Factory's driveway

Once you have the Voodoo, drive toward the pink blip to meet Rico and the other Cubans in the parking lot across from Kaufman Cabs. Follow Rico and his comrades to the pink marker located in an alley half a block away.

The Haitians open the front gate and let all the cars in. As you drive into the compound, run over as many of the Haitians as you can, while still posing as one of them. This will lessen the numbers once you're out of the car.

Park the car in the pink marker and enter the factory. Walk into the three blips inside the factory to plant bombs (one is located on the second level and requires a little stair climbing). When you're done, get out of the factory before it blows. You'll have only 20 seconds to escape after the first bomb is planted, so be quick about it.

The gate you passed to enter the compound is closed, and now that your cover is blown, driving a Voodoo will not make them open the gate. Facing the closed gate, head right (south) and run up the stairs in the narrow alley behind the building. Run across the rooftop of the next building and excape onto the streets. Once you're out, you'll get some pyrotechnics from the factory and $10,000 in reward money.

Umberto Call
After you complete his last mission, Umberto calls on the cell phone just to thank you for the bang-up job you did on the factory.

TROJAN VOODOO

BOATYARD

Boatyard Mission

CHECKPOINT CHARLIE

There's a bunch of packages out in the water, just waiting to be acquired. Hop in your snazzy new speedboat, courtesy of your own personal Boatyard (cost: $10,000), and collect them all within the time limit. You have two boats to choose from, the Squallo or the Cuban Jetmax. The Squallo is faster, but you may find the Jetmax easier to handle.

The usual warnings apply—control your turns, hit the jumps fast, and be careful in tight areas. Complete the mission once and then try it again, and so on. Every time you complete the challenge, the prize increases by $1000. However, the challenge gets tougher as the air becomes foggier; by the fourth challenge, it's almost impossible to see.

💲 **Payoff:** No cash reward. Complete this challenge for the Boatyard Asset, plus the mission rewards.

❓ **Description:** Collect the floating packages with your speedboat.

KAUFMAN CABS

Serving Vice City 24 hours

Kaufman Cab Missions

V.I.P.

Purchase Kaufman Cabs and the Taxi Missions immediately become available. Just make sure that you're in a Kaufman Cab when entering the pink marker inside the Taxi garage.

> **$ Payoff: $1000**
>
> **? Description:** Teach a rival taxi a lesson in manners by pounding his fare-stealing cab into twisted metal, then deliver your rightful customer to the airport.

There's a VIP on Starfish Island that needs a lift. Drive over there quickly (you have only one minute), then stop and blare the horn while in the marker.

Suddenly another Taxi pulls up and tries to steal your fare—you're not going to stand for that, are you? Chase him down and get the VIP back. Use multiple collisions or drive-by shootings. After a certain amount of damage, the passenger exits your rival's taxi.

Drive up to the fare and allow him to enter your cab. Once you have him in your car, take him to his destination at Escobar International Airport.

You'll earn $1000 for completing this mission.

FRIENDLY RIVALRY

MISSION

$ Payoff: $2000

? Description: Gain market share by destroying the competition.

VC Cabs is stealing your fares. If your cab company is going to prosper, you need to get rid of the competition.

Track down three of the VC Cabs (following the yellow blips on the map) and destroy them. Drive-by shooting is the easiest way to accomplish this. When you near them, they will try to ram you, but not too agressively. This works to your benefit, because you won't have to chase them all over town. When they ram you, shoot them.

You'll earn $2000 for completing this mission.

CABMAGEDDON

Mercedes wants a little personal attention, so pick her up pronto... or maybe not.

Payoff: $3000
(plus $5000/day income and a Zebra Cab parked at Kaufman Cabs)

Description: Survive an attack from VC Cab and defeat their boss.

When you arrive at the pickup point and sound the horn, a host of the rival, VC Cab, shows up and starts a makeshift demolition derby. Unfortunately, you're the target.

Drive into 8-ball's bomb shop (one of the last blue garage doors near the water) and the cabs will follow you in. After the door closes and opens again, your cab will be rigged to explode. Exit the car and jump over the swarming cabs, then exit 8-ball's. Detonate the cab-bomb and all the rival taxis will go up with it.

Stay alive for one minute and the VC leader cab will show up. Since you're now without a car, shoot the Zebra Cab's tires to slow it down. When it tries to run you over, jump over it, then run up to the cab, pull the driver out, and kill him—run him over with his own cab! Destroy it to complete the mission successfully and earn yourself a daily income of $5000, plus $3000 in your pocket immediately, and a new cab parked in Kaufman Cabs.

THE MALIBU

Malibu Missions

NO ESCAPE?

After acquiring The Malibu, head inside and enter the pink marker on the opposite side of the dance floor. Tommy spends some time talking to Rosenberg about getting a new employee—a safe cracker. Tommy has something big in mind.

Oh, all right, well, let me think...safe, safe, safe, safe – I got it! This guy will blow you away!

Payoff: $1000

Description: Bust Cam Jones, the safe-cracker, out of jail.

The man you want, Cam Jones, is in police custody—and you're going to spring him.

Head for the Vice City police department, park a strong but quick vehicle near the stairs, then go inside. Make sure your weapons aren't selected, or the cops will get a bit skittish with you.

WASHINGTON BEACH

Cam's House

LITTLE HAVANA

Pay'n'Spray

The key card to the cells can be found upstairs in the station.

Suit up in a police uniform from the locker room on the left to get upstairs without being hassled. This is where you'll find the keycard you need to get Jones out of the lockup.

Go down to the basement, then enter the pink marker to use the key card on the cell lock and free Jones. Unfortunately, you'll also trigger a four star Wanted Level. You must get both yourself and Jones to safety to finish the mission. Take your time moving through each room while popping the cops. Keep an eye on your back; the law files into the station from a back door.

Once the two of you are safely inside your vehicle, quickly find the nearest Pay 'n' Spray to lose the Wanted Level. When Jones gets home, you'll get $1000 and Jones' services for an upcoming mission.

THE SHOOTIST

Consulting with Rosenberg again on the subject of someone who can handle a gun doesn't turn up much, but Jones knows a man named Phil Cassidy who might fit the bill.

💲 **Payoff:** $2000

❓ **Description:** Prove you can shoot better than Phil Cassidy and he'll join your criminal team.

Follow the pink blip to the Downtown Ammu-Nation to meet with Cassidy. Once inside, enter the pink marker in front of the doorway that leads to the back of the store.

Cassidy will challenge you to an impromptu-shooting contest. You need to hit more targets than he does within the two-minute time limit. Running out of ammunition also ends the round. Hitting the closest target nets you a point; the middle distance targets two points; and the furthest, three.

The points are awarded only after the whole target dummy is destroyed (head and all quadrants). Concentrate your fire on the furthest target more than the closer two. Shoot the closer two targets when they pass your sights or when waiting for the furthest to regenerate—since the most distant target nets you the most points.

Next up, head over to the urban target zone in the back room of the Ammu-Nation. This time, any target is worth one point. Try concentrating on only two windows (one above the other) instead of continually aiming at all the windows when a target appears. This technique saves you time you would waste chasing targets that you'd never hit.

Mysterious Call

Upon completion of this mission, you receive a cell phone call from a mysterious caller. He wants you to head to the payphone in Little Havana. Taking the caller up on this request will allow you to finish the final Assassin Mission, "Loose Ends" (see page 91).

Walk forward into the next blip that appears in the same room when the second round ends to start another urban target range—same time limit, same scoring.

In total, you need to beat 60 points. If you do, Cassidy will agree to work for you, and you'll earn $2000.

THE DRIVER

One more component is needed to complete your squad of crooks— the driver. The goal is to convince a guy named Hillary to get behind the wheel for you. He'll agree only if you can beat him in a race.

$ Payoff: $3000

? Description: Beat Hillary at his own game—driving fast—and he'll go to work for you.

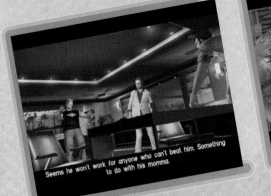

Seems he won't work for anyone who can't beat him. Something to do with his momma.

You Tommy? Of course you're Tommy, I mean,

There's no time limit here, just a normal checkpoint race—oh, except that the cops will be pursuing both of you with a two-star Wanted Level. Unfortunately, you don't get to choose your car; to be fair, you're given a Sentinel. It's a pretty tough race to win—you can only hope that Hillary gets nailed by oncoming traffic or slowed by the cops. You can try bumping him and spinning him out, but this usually just causes you more trouble than him. Keep the pedal to the metal and aim for the outer edge of the markers when traffic gets thick inside the checkpoints. Use sidewalks when necessary to avoid cops and other cars.

Avoid the law and finish the race ahead of Hillary to earn $3000 and a new driver.

THE JOB

We walk into the bank, we wave the gun around, and leave very rich men.

With all the components assembled, it's finally time to hit the bank. Hop in the taxi waiting outside with the rest of your team. The gang consists of Cam on the safe, Phil and yourself as lookouts, and Hillary as the getaway car driver.

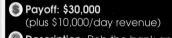
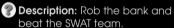

💲 **Payoff: $30,000**
(plus $10,000/day revenue)

❓ **Description:** Rob the bank and beat the SWAT team.

Make sure everyone on the team gets in the cab before it leaves, then follow the pink blip to the bank in Little Havana. Leave the vehicle, and Hillary will take it around the block to wait for the three of you to emerge from the bank.

Lead the guys across the street and walk up the steps of the bank. Enter the pink marker to the right of the entrance and your team will change outfits. Now you can enter the bank.

So far, so good—Phil will watch the people in the bank's lobby while you and Cam go upstairs to the vault. Several guards will attack you up there, so be ready for them. There's some Armor on the second floor if you need it.

Cruel and Unusual Punishment

Since the SWAT team storms the bank no matter what you do, executing all the employees and security guards inside the bank before triggering the SWAT invasion is one way to avoid accidentally targeting them when the SWAT shootout begins. Targeting and shooting them during the shootout could cost you dearly when you need to stay alive. Shooting them before this event happens will make targeting the SWAT members much easier and you won't waste time on someone who isn't a threat. However, if you go this route, you'll have to go all the way and waste everyone, or else they will beat Cam to death, and you'll fail the mission.

Ride the elevator and make sure Jones is with you, then leave him at the safe. He complains that it will take too long, so head back down the elevator to find the manager in a second floor office—he's cowering in a corner behind his desk. Don't run. Allow the manager to follow you into the elevator, then take him back upstairs with you.

This could take hours to crack.

Leave the manager with Jones and return to the lobby—the alarm has been sounded, and you have a three-star Wanted Level. Enter the pink marker behind the desk, near the front entrance of the bank. Jones opens the vault about now, but you have to deal with the incoming SWAT team first.

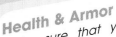

Run behind the desk near the stairs and use it as cover. Fire a submachine gun or the one-shot-kills from the Magnum and target the SWAT team gunners, one after the other, as they drop in from the ventilation ducts. Once the area is clear, a pink marker appears at the front doors. Enter it when you're ready to confront the masses waiting for you outside.

Once outside, Hillary pulls up in the escape vehicle, and is shot by the heat. Shoot only the authorities that are an immediate threat (ones that could quickly open the doors to the cab once you enter it), then hop in the cab as quickly as possible. If Phil is killed, the mission will fail; you need him alive to finish the game.

Now you just have to get back alive. Reach the nearby Pay 'n' Spray, then head for home. $30,000 in cash is your reward, and The Malibu now generates revenue of $10,000, in addition to opening up Phil's missions.

Health & Armor

Make sure that you take full advantage of the Health and Armor in the bank before venturing outside. The Armor is located in the security monitoring room (you can walk up to the monitors and see what's happening all over the bank), and the Health is in the manager's office.

Phil Calls

After the bank job goes down, Phil calls on the cell phone and offers his assistance with anything you need. This event opens Phil's missions.

Bank Job Outfit

After completing the bank job, the Bank Job Outfit is delivered to the Malibu Club in Vice Point. Excellent!

PHIL

CASSIDY

Phil's Missions

GUN RUNNER

Follow the large **P** icon on the radar to locate Phil's Place in Little Haiti. Tommy stops by to inquire about some weaponry, and Phil mentions a Mexican gunrunner who passes through town. He wants you to go and liberate some of his goods. To do this, you need to track down his trucks and ram the goods out of them.

Hop in the Patriot and follow one of the four yellow blips on your radar to reach one of the trucks. When the yellow blips first appear, the trucks are very close to one another, so it appears to be only two blips. Use the Drive-by technique to tear up the trucks and shoot the gunners from the beds of their trucks. After dealing a fair amount of damage, the trucks will drop one weapon each. Once it's on the ground, ram the crate (if it survived the mayhem) and pick up the weapon, then find the next truck.

> **$ Payoff: $2000**
> **? Description:** Ram four gunrunner trucks into dropping their weapons cargo, then destroy the vehicles and their drivers.

Eliminate all the Runners

Finish off all the occupants inside the trucks as you pick up each dropped weapon. If you don't, they'll just follow you around town as you chase the next target, causing you major trouble. You really don't need more thugs on your tail as you attack subsequent gunrunners.

Cool the Heat

If you get yourself a high Wanted Level or if the Patroit is taking a beating, take a break in the middle of the mission to hit a Pay 'n' Spray.

Phil Calls

After completing this mission, Phil calls you on the cell phone and offers you some of his Boomshine. This unlocks Phil's final mission!

Collect all four weapons from the four trucks and get rid of the arms dealer to finish the mission and earn another $2000.

Tommy, it's Phil, now cut all the reminiscing crap and listen to me, you hear?

P Phil's Place

STARFISH IS

Hospital

Surgeon

BOOMSHINE SAIGON

Tommy visits an inebriated Phil, who manages to blow his own arm off— now you know why he was missing that limb in Grand Theft Auto 3!

$ **Payoff:** $4000

? **Description:** Get Phil some medical attention quickly!

man it smells like paint stripper. Making my eyes burn...

You must get him to the hospital before he bleeds to death (keep an eye on Phil's Health Meter below your Wanted Level). You have about one minute and thirty seconds to complete the mission.

This task is complicated somewhat by the Boomshine that Tommy inhaled, so he's not going to do too well on the road. Steer very carefully. Your controls are hypersensitive, which can quickly lead to some massive over-steering.

When you finally reach the hospital, Phil protests. Too many cops, of course. He directs you to an ex-army surgeon down in Little Havana.

Follow the blip and drop Phil off with his shady primary care physician to finish the mission. You'll earn yourself $4000, Phil's Place, and access to some very cool new weapons there. Phil, on the other hand, un-earns himself an arm.

Phil's health:

Phil's health:

PHILS PLACE ASSET COMPLETED!

Not the hospital, man! Too many cops and Viet Cong!

COUNTERFEITING PRINT WORKS

Print Works

Print Works Missions

SPILLING THE BEANS

- **Payoff:** $2000
- **Description:** Extract some information from a Shipping Officer at the docks.

Once you purchase the Print Works for $70,000, the Print Works missions become available.

Your first job in the string of counterfeit money operations ultimately leads to a direct confrontation with the mob. For now, though, you've got matters of more immediate concern.

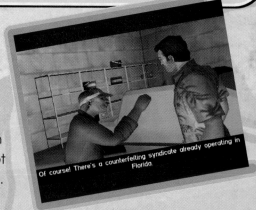

Of course! There's a counterfeiting syndicate already operating in Florida.

The old man who works at the Print Works says he could probably print up some decent counterfeit cash, but he needs a good set of plates to do it. Tommy heads off to talk with Kent Paul about finding just such a set. Hop into the Kaufman Cab outside the Print Works and hitch a ride to The Malibu. Once there, Tommy strikes up a conversation with Kent Paul and mentions that the Triads deal with them.

You can use this Kaufman Cab to take you to destinations instead of driving. It will cost you $9.

They've got a shipping company down the docks.

Leave The Malibu and you're directed to the Chartered Libertine Lines boat at the docks in Viceport. Jack a car and head down to the docks, using the pink blip to guide you. There's a Shipping Officer that you need to speak with.

The guy you're looking for is up on the Chartered Libertine ship parked at the docks, but you'll be shot on sight, so be ready for a firefight when you board the boat. Use the Armor across the street from the ship if you aren't already prepared for flying lead.

Map labels: The Print Works · Cab to Malibu · STARFISH ISLAND · Kent Paul reveals Plate location · WASHINGTON BEACH · LITTLE HAVANA · Plates aboard this ship · Pay 'n' Spray

Follow the blip on the radar to the north end of the ship and climb the stairs to the third level. The pink marker is in front of a guarded doorway. Enter it after eliminating the threat.

Extracting the info from the Shipping Officer gets you a two-star Wanted Level, and you need to get back to the Print Works in one piece. Use the Health power-up below the stairs you used to board the ship and replenish any lost health, then speed off to the Pay 'n' Spray located south of your position to lose the Wanted Level. Follow the pink blip on the radar back to the Print Works and you'll earn $2000 for your troubles.

HIT THE COURIER

Step two in your string of counterfeiting jobs requires you to intercept the courier with the plates. She'll arrive via helicopter at the docks.

- 💲 **Payoff: $5,000** (plus $8,000 revenue from the Print Works)
- ❓ **Description:** Gun down the courier delivering the plates you need for counterfeiting.

Get down to the docks and wait just outside. When the courier lands, she'll get in a car and drive off. While waiting for the courier to enter her vehicle, use the sniper rifle to pick off as many of the lady assassins in the highly guarded shipyard from a vantage point just outside the gates. Start with the sniper on the rooftop—she can cause you some major hurt. Next, snipe the tires of the cars that the courier and the assassins will enter. Blowing out the tires will make catching the fleeing vehicle very easy.

Intercept the courier's vehicle, defeat her, and retrieve the plates (yellow blip on the radar).

Get them back to the Print Works and you'll earn $5000, plus the $8000 revenue from the Print Works.

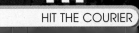

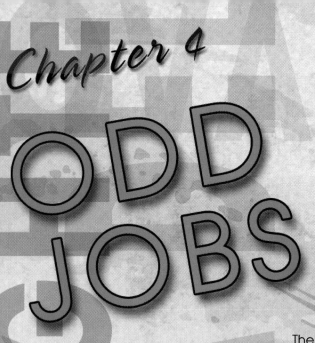

Chapter 4
ODD JOBS

There's a lot of fun (and cash) to be had around the city that doesn't directly involve the main story. Various property missions are also available to you. You can go racing, flying, or leaping across Vice City, get in a demolition derby (not involving cabs), and all kinds of other goodies. Take a glance through this section to see what's out there, and enjoy these activities when you're in the mood for something different.

Many of the Odd Jobs reward you with a low cash payout at first. This amount increases each time you manage to beat the record (usually your own), so it is possible to pocket a good stack of green if you feel like playing one of these games for a while. The Odd Jobs must be completed to reach 100% completion of the game.

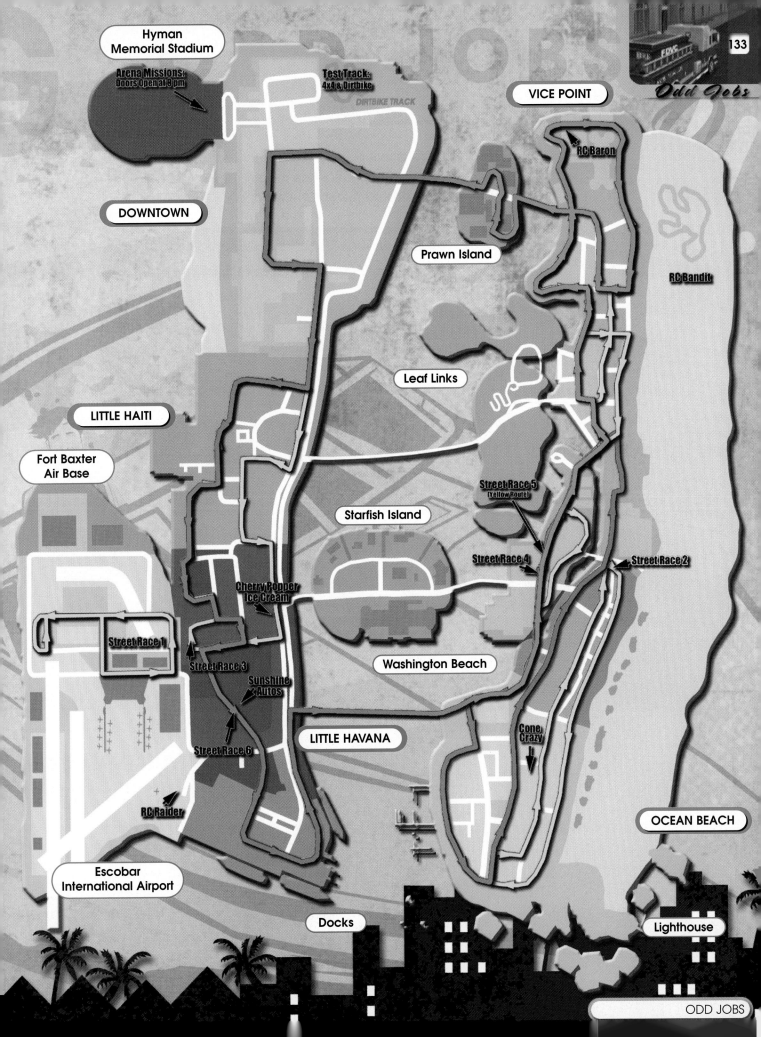

Hyman Memorial Stadium

Arena Missions: Doors Open at 8 pm

Test Track: 4x4 & Dirtbike

DIRTBIKE TRACK

VICE POINT

RC Baron

DOWNTOWN

Prawn Island

RC Bandit

LITTLE HAITI

Leaf Links

Fort Baxter Air Base

Starfish Island

Street Race 5 (Yellow Route)

Street Race 4

Street Race 2

Cherry Popper Ice Cream

Street Race 1

Street Race 3

Washington Beach

Sunshine Autos

LITTLE HAVANA

Cone Crazy

Street Race 6

RC Raider

OCEAN BEACH

Escobar International Airport

Docks

Lighthouse

The Cherry Popper Ice Cream Mission

Purchase the Cherry Popper Ice Cream Factory in Little Havana for $20,000 to open your own personal "ice cream" delivery service. Once the Distribution is complete, the Cherry Popper will generate $3000 per day.

Sales Strategy

To unlock the Cherry Popper daily Asset, you must have 50 sales during one mission; this means not getting busted, wasted, or exiting the Mr. Whoopee truck. Try selling to a few customers and then relocating to another street to make a few more deals elsewhere. This will keep the cops at a distance until you've sold enough to complete the mission. There's also an abundance of "ice cream" hungry citizens in the Docks area of Viceport, which is close to the Pay 'n' Spray. Try to keep your Wanted Level below 2.

DISTRIBUTION

Use your ice cream truck (Mr. Whoopee) to distribute "treats" to the locals around town.

When you stop and turn on the music (L3), all nearby junkies flock to your truck to get their fix. Unfortunately, the more you sell, the more the fuzz will get after you.

Keep selling and you'll wind up with the military on your tail—not a good thing. How much you earn depends on just how many sales you manage to rack up before bailing out from the heat. Keep in mind that some gangs don't like you pushing in their neighborhood, and will come after you.

Money received for each transaction depends on where you sell the product.

DISTRICT	AMOUNT RECEIVED PER SELL
Airport	$12
Starfish Island	$18
Prawn Island	$14
Little Havana	$8
Little Haiti	$8
All Others	$10

Car Showroom Missions

VICE CITY STREET RACES

The Street Races are checkpoint competitions. You can compete in each race as many times as you wish to better your best time around the course. If you're in the mood for speed, then stop by your showroom, head down to the garages, and enter the pink marker near the Vice City wall map. Press the Directional Pad to select the different courses, then press the X Button to confirm your choice. This Street Race map also keeps track of your personal bests. Your competitors will drive a Stinger, Infernus, and a Cheetah in all six races.

Car Showroom purchased: $40000

B.J. Smith. And you must be Mr. Vercetti.

Cheetah

> **Sunshine Autos**
> Purchasing Sunshine Autos from BJ Smith for $50,000 opens a set of street races, and also allows you to begin a car-stealing spree. Completing the car-jacking jobs ultimately results in free and legal cars for the taking. Also, the Pay 'n' Spray on the premises will offer free paint jobs, and you'll have access to four garages, which store/save two vehicles each.

RACE #1: TERMINAL VELOCITY

The first race is a 1.1-mile run with a $400 reward. It costs $100 to enter and takes place on the mainland, between Fort Baxter and the airport. Each time you win this race, you'll receive $400.

Street Race 1

VICE STREET RACER
EARN CASH, NOT KUDOS

Race 1:
Terminal Velocity
Track Length: 1.1 miles
Entrance Fee: $100

Best Time: NA
Best Result: NA

RACE #2: OCEAN DRIVE

The second race is a 1.6-mile run along Ocean Beach. You'll earn $2000 for completing this long, thin loop with a hairpin at each end. The entrance fee is $500. Each time you win this race, you'll receive $2000.

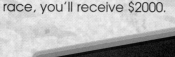

RACE #3: BORDER RUN

This 2-mile race takes place in midtown on the mainland. It has a decent purse of $4000 for the winner. The entrance fee is $1000. Each time you win the race, you'll receive $4000.

RACE #4: CAPITAL CRUISE

This lengthy race is 2.438 miles, stretching from the southernmost part of Ocean Beach all the way up to Washington Beach. Taking the gold will earn you a nice $8000, which more than makes up for the $2000 entrance fee. Each time you win this race, you'll receive $8000.

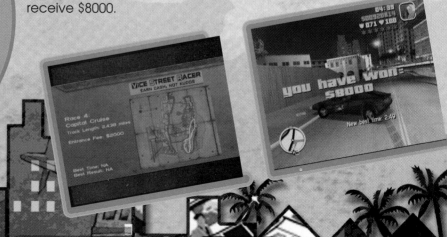

Odd Jobs

RACE #5: TOUR!

A very extensive track, at nearly 3 miles, this course runs from northern Vice Point into mid-Washington Beach. Finishing it first generates a hefty $20,000. The entrance fee is $5000. Each time you win this race, you'll earn $20,000.

RACE #6: V.C. ENDURANCE

Just like the name says, this is, by far, the longest track. It also affords the most room for mistakes, and awards the largest purse: $40,000. If you manage to claim the lead and keep a steady hand on the steering wheel, you can cruise your way around the whole city and hit the finish line first. The length of the race is 6.1 miles and the entrance fee is a whopping $10,000! Each time you win this race, you'll receive $40,000.

ROAD HAZZARDS
While it is possible to switch cars during the race, you'll lose a lot of time doing so. Also, watch out for undue police attention—they can really ruin your day.

VICE CITY STREET RACES

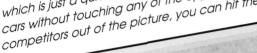

Alternative Racing Strategy

All the Vice City races have one thing in common: the competitors can be taken out of the race before it even begins with a couple well-placed Rocket Launcher shells. Pick up this powerful weapon from the pool behind the Hooker Hotel, which is just a quick drive from the Showroom. Bring it to the starting line, then shell the pavement between two of the sports cars without touching any of the opponents' vehicles. When the third car tries to begin the race, let him have it! With all the competitors out of the picture, you can hit the checkpoints with a vehicle as slow as the Faggio!

STOLEN CARS

Once you own the Car Showroom, head down to the lower garages behind the building and you'll find a list of cars on the wall near a single garage (near the Street Race Map). The first list requires a certain type of stolen vehicle. Once that list is complete, your prize vehicle appears inside the showroom. A second list then appears on the wall, and so on, until all four lists are complete. The following list details the cars needed for each list, and which vehicle is unlocked after fulfilling the requests.

GARAGE 1	GARAGE 2	GARAGE 3	GARAGE 4
Landstalker	Sabre	Cheetah	Voodoo
Idaho	Virgo	Infernus	Cuban Hermes
Esperanto	Sentinel	Banshee	Caddy
Stallion	Stretch	Phoenix	Baggage Handler
Rancher	Washington	Comet	Mr. Whoopee
Blista Compact	Admiral	Stinger	Pizza Boy
Reward Car: Deluxo	**Reward Car:** Sabre Turbo	**Reward Car:** Sandking	**Reward Car:** Hotring Racer

RC Missions

Several Top Fun vans are scattered around town, and each one accesses a different type of RC mission. There's a car, a helicopter, and a plane checkpoint race. You'll earn $100 for completing these missions, and $100 more if you beat your own time.

Self Destruct Button

The Circle Button detonates any type of RC vehicle. This is useful if you want to quit the challenge.

RC BANDIT CHECKPOINT RACE

A lonely Top Fun van is parked on the beach. Hop in for some RC car action on the sandy track. You must complete two laps around the track and finish in first place to win. Don't hesitate to skip over a section of the track if you can, but avoid over-steering on the loose surface.

Finishing first earns you $100. Okay, so it's not a huge cash outlay, but it was still fun, right?

Cornering is Key

Tapping on the Handbrake in all sharp turns is critical to completing the course in the least amount of time.

RC BARON CHECKPOINT RACE

There's another Toy Fun van on the top floor of the large carpark next to the North Point Mall in Vice Point. This one gives you control of the RC Baron, a tiny bi-plane. Three other mini bi-planes compete with you for domination of the single lap checkpoint course. Watch out for stoplights and trees while flying low to the ground and you should finish first, but don't miss any checkpoints on the way. When flying the RC bi-planes, do not release the X Button (Gas) or you'll dive, and recovery is difficult. The L2 and R2 Buttons control left and right yaw. To dive, press up on the Left Analog Stick. To climb, press down.

As before, you'll earn $100 for finishing first.

RC RAIDER CHECKPOINT PICKUP

Go to the airport to find the last isolated Top Fun van. This one gives you control of the RC Raider, a mini helicopter. Your objective is a bit different this time. You must pass through 20 checkpoints scattered around the airport. The difficulty comes from the fragility of your craft. Delicately maneuver into the tight spaces, or you'll bang up the tiny helicopter and destroy it before you can finish.

As you pass through one checkpoint, the pink blip on the radar directs you to the next. The final checkpoint is the toughest one to find. It's tucked away between shipping containers, under the shelter near the Top Fun van. No need to go under the shelter, just head to the south side of it and drop down near the blue container to pick up the final checkpoint. You'll get another $100 for finishing in time.

A second Dirt Track is located along the northern
coast of the mainland. Here you
have a choice of Dirt Bike action
with the Sanchez, or some solid 4x4
driving in the Landstalker. The
object is to romp over the track and
hit all the checkpoints. Each time
you complete two laps of the track,
you earn some money. Beat your
previous time and chalk up even
more cash.

LANDSTALKER (4X4) TEST TRACK

Use your stability to go up and over the terrain and reach the checkpoints.
You won't be able to manage much speed, but given that you are only
competing against yourself, this isn't much of a problem. Be careful on the
rugged turns, as the Landstalker is top-heavy and may tip
over—this is largest challenge to overcome.
Use the Handbrake in the
sharp turns to keep slow-
downs to a minimum from
normal braking. You will
receive $100 x the number
of successful attempts on
this course.

SANCHEZ (DIRT BIKE) TRIAL BY DIRT

You'll have a lot more speed with the Sanchez bike, but at the expense of
the stability enjoyed in the 4x4. You must actually follow the track and
watch out for the obstacles on the course.

Rain is guaranteed to fall on this course just after beginning the challenge.
The slippery ground isn't your only distraction, however, once armed thugs
on dirt bikes enter the picture. Pack an Uzi for this challenge and shoot the
thugs before they knock you off the bike. Falling from the Sanchez may
cause you to fail the challenge if you can't get back on in time.
You may even end up in the hospital if you
don't draw first blood. You will
receive $100 x the num-
ber of successful attempts
on this course.

Arena Missions

Located northwest of Downtown mainland, the Hyman Memorial Stadium opens every evening at 8:00 (20:00) and features three different types of Stadium motor sports. Only one particular event is featured each day. One day it's the Bloodring, the next it's Dirtring, and the third day it's the Hotring. These events continue back-to-back throughout the entire week. Glance up at the banner above the doors to see which event is being featured that night. Head up the large set of stairs to the main entrance, wait for the doors to open at 20:00, and then enter to get the fun started!

BLOODRING

Drive through the checkpoints that appear, one after the other, around the arena to increase your overall time. You will fail if your overall time reaches zero. Get your overall time above the target time to win. The first target time is one minute.

Keep moving toward the target as the others try to keep you away from it. Use reverse, if necessary, to continue moving toward the checkpoint after being spun and kicked around. The surface of the arena floor is dirt, and the biggest challenge is overcoming your vehicle's tendency to slide across the surface. Keep in mind that when you ram an opponent's vehicle, the car you hit is taking the damage. If an opponent rams you, your vehicle takes the damage. Use the different views (L2 and R2) to keep an eye on the closest bangers. You'll earn $1000 for completing this challenge, plus a $100 bonus for each car destroyed (not necessarily caused by you). You will receive $1000 for each stage passed.

DIRTRING

In the Dirtring, you are given a Sanchez (Dirt Bike) to complete the course by passing through all the checkpoints. If you want to leave the stadium, get off the bike and enter the pink marker. There are 32 checkpoints to hit and it's no easy task to get some of them, even with unlimited time.

The tougher checkpoints are on top of thin, broken walls or beyond a narrow wooden plank. Make sure to line yourself up perfectly with the narrow edge, then do not adjust your steering once you're on that surface. More speed usually helps in these challenges, enabling you to sail through distant checkpoints.

The toughest checkpoint on the Dirt Bike requires you to do a perfectly-timed wheelie through it; you cannot simply ride through it with both tires on the ground.

You receive $50,000 each time you complete the Dirtring challenge in less than five minutes, $10,000 for each time you pass it in less than ten minutes, or $5000 for each time the mission is passed in over ten minutes.

HOTRING

The Hotring is a Nascar-style race where demolition is encouraged (as if it's not in Nascar). The race lasts for 12 laps. Only first, second, and third place qualify for winnings. If your car is destroyed, you will be disqualified. When your car is damaged, you can get it repaired at the pit stop, but you risk losing the lead. If you want out of the challenge, exit your vehicle and enter door near the starting position. Drive-by shooting is still an option for getting ahead of the competition. Avoid other cars as much as possible to keep your health up for the duration of the race, and ignore pit stops to maintain your lead. You receive $5000 for each time you finish first, $1500 for second place, and $500 for third.

Cone Crazy

A test of your driving finesse, this mission requires you to hit five checkpoints in any order. The timer starts counting down when you hit the first checkpoint.

The catch is, you can't touch a single cone or you'll fail the mission. Drive carefully—each cone gives you just 12 seconds on the clock. You get $200 for completing this mission the first time. This total doubles each subsequent time you complete the challenge.

The trick is to reach the two Checkpoint markers on the Unique Jump ramp on the southwest corner of the rooftop first. Just drive up the ramp and turn sharply into the second checkpoint on your way down the other side of the ramp without hitting the cones up there. This will give you a quick extra 24 seconds. This is enough time to reach the east checkpoint, the middle checkpoint, and then finally the one near the starting position.

Pizza Delivery

Hop on the pizza bike to trigger this mini game. You must deliver your load of pizzas before the time expires. You can throw a pizza to the customer by doing a drive-by. Unload all the pizzas in time, or else a rival pizza place will get the order. When you need some more pizzas, return to the pizza store and restock.

Each time you make a delivery, the number of pizzas you must deliver increases. You'll start out with six pizzas, and only a single order (so you can miss a few). However, if you do that in time and return for more orders, you must then make two deliveries with six pizzas, then three with six, four with six, and so on. Your margin for error shrinks with every successful delivery—and the five-minute time limit remains the same each time. You receive $10 for each pizza delivered and $5000 for completion of the strand of deliveries.

> **150 MAX HEALTH**
> Complete Level 10 to unlock Max Health of 150hp. Each time you pick up a Health icon, it will fill your health to a maximum of 150hp. **!**

Taxi Driver

Hop in any taxi and press the R3 Button to begin the Taxi Driver job. Pick up a fare, follow the radar blip to the fare's destination, drop 'em off, and then collect some coinage. Deliver them quickly to get speed bonuses! However, don't drive too recklessly or the fare will bail. Also, if your ride is too much of a wreck, the fare will not even enter the vehicle. The amount received from these missions is proportional to the distance covered and the amount of time it took to get there.

BOOST UNLOCK
Deliver 100 fares to unlock the Boost! Once you have a fair amount of acceleration, "Boost" allows all cab-type vehicles to perform a hydraulic jump by pressing the L3 Button.

Kaufman Coffin
Kaufman Cabs roll over so easily, even with just a moderate amount of speed and normal turning, that you should consider using the Taxi and not the Kaufman Cab when attempting the Taxi Driver job.

PARAMEDIC, VIGILANTE, AND FIRE TRUCK MISSION JOB REWARDS

Level 1:	$50	Level 7:	$2450
Level 2:	$200	Level 8:	$3200
Level 3:	$450	Level 9:	$4050
Level 4:	$800	Level 10:	$5000
Level 5:	$1250	Level 11:	$6050
Level 6:	$1800	Level 12:	$7200

Paramedic

Hop in an ambulance to trigger this mission type whenever you want—just press the R3 Button.

You'll receive a call for an ambulance at a specified location. You must then get there in time and deliver the patient (intact) to a hospital to complete one run.

The longer you can maintain a streak, the tougher it gets—more patients need to be picked up—and the higher the paramedic level you can reach.

INFINITE SPRINT
Reach, and complete, Level 12 of the Paramedic Mission to unlock Infinite Sprint. As with GTA III, this allows Tommy to continue to run nonstop without becoming winded.

Vigilante

Hop in a law enforcement vehicle to trigger the Vigilante missions (check out our Vehicle Showroom in the *Welcome to Vice City* section of this guide for a complete list of Vigilante vehicles). You'll receive a target and a time limit. Track down the target and destroy it to complete a single run.

Every target you eliminate gives you more time on the clock, so you can continue for quite some time if you keep your car in one piece. The longer you stay on the job, the higher your Vigilante level. The higher the level, the more criminals there are to track down (vehicle numbers increase, as well as the number of criminals in those vehicles).

BROWN THUNDER

Collect all 100 Hidden Packages and claim the secret vehicle from the Air Base. When you find it (you can't miss it), press the R3 Button to begin the Vigilante mission, "Brown Thunder." Not only is this mission a blast, but you may also find it easier to reach Level 12 in this secret vehicle than running around on the ground with an automobile.

Quick Change
You can hop out of your cruiser briefly to use weapons or switch to another law enforcement vehicle if necessary.

150 ARMOR
Reach, and complete, Level 12 of the Vigilante Mission to unlock 150 Armor. This increases your Body Armor max to 150. All Armor power-ups will put you at 150!

Fire Truck

Grab the Fire Truck from the Downtown station, or just start your own fire somewhere and jack one of these big red trucks, then press the R3 Button to begin the Fire Fighter mission. Press the L3 Button to use the siren and some cars will get out of your way. Cruise around and, before long, car fires will begin to appear on the radar. Use the Circle Button to spray from the front of the truck, and use the gas and reverse buttons to aim the water onto the burning cars. When the occupants escape (after squirting the vehicle), douse them to complete the level. Higher levels bring more cars and more burning people that run from them.

FIREPROOF
Reach, and complete, Level 12 of the Fire Truck Mission to unlock Fireproof. This allows you to run through fire without taking damage!

PCJ Playground

Collect 24 checkpoints in the two-minute time limit, which starts when you hit the first checkpoint.

It's pretty simple, except that you're on a PCJ 600—and many of the checkpoints are on top of buildings!

Maintain careful control of your bike through the jumps and between the narrow alleys to finish in time. You'll get a cool $1000 for completing the race. Beat your time on your next attempt to receive another $1000, and so on.

Chopper Checkpoint Races

Four helicopters are scattered throughout Vice City and within your reach. Enter one to trigger a checkpoint mission over the city. As with the RC races, you are competing against your own best time. You'll receive $100 each time you play and successfully pass each mission.

To move forward in a helicopter, you must first give it some gas and a little altitude, then press up slightly on the Right Analog Stick. If you continue to press up all the way, you will point the nose of the Sparrow at a dangerous angle and eventually hit the ground. Pressing slightly forward gives you safe (albeit slow) and even forward movement. Continue to hold the X Button or you'll lose lift. If you want to go faster, bring the nose down, but make sure to also let up occasionally to climb. Pressing down on the Control Stick backs you out of tight situations, but if you want to go in the opposite direction, use the rudder blade (L2 and R2) to turn the bird around and face the other direction. Backward is not an effective direction of flight in any kind of aircraft.

FLIGHT CONTROLS

 LT | **UP** Forward Movement

 LT | **DN** Backward Movement

 Gas

 Decrease Altitude

 Bail Out

R2 Tail Movement Right (left turn)

L2 Tail Movement Left (right turn)

Chopper Checkpoints

Little Haiti, Ocean Beach, and Vice Point Chopper Checkpoints open after the "Rub Out" mission. Coincidentally, the Maverick is awarded after Rub Out. It can be found on Tommy's estate and on top of the Hyman Condo. The Downtown Chopper Checkpoint opens after the "G-Spotlight" Mission.

OCEAN BEACH CHOPPER CHECKPOINT

This Sparrow is located on a pink rooftop—the same building where you end the PCJ Playground challenge. Jump in to begin the Ocean Beach Chopper Checkpoint challenge. The key to victory is avoiding buildings, trees, and other solid objects. Keep your chopper healthy while securing checkpoints to maintain sufficient altitude, and use the Square Button to descend onto the checkpoint (in tight areas) while hovering above it. Use the blips on the radar to find all the checkpoints and you'll earn $100.

LITTLE HAITI CHOPPER CHECKPOINT

The Little Haiti Chopper Checkpoint challenge is located on a rooftop in Little Haiti (just beyond a Police Bribe and Unique Jump alley ramp). Enter the Sparrow and fly around Little Haiti, picking up the 22 checkpoints. This challenge is not as tough as the others—most of the checkpoints are in the open and do not require any fancy maneuvers.

VICE POINT CHOPPER CHECKPOINT

The Sparrow that initiates the Vice Point Chopper Checkpoint challenge is located in a backyard of a quaint little neighborhood. The first four checkpoints you go through will have you dodging one palm tree after another. After that, however, it gets easier. You'll fly around the North Point Mall and head back toward town. There are only 17 checkpoints in this challenge, but the obstacles more than make up for that. Collect $100 the first time through, and then try to beat your time and see how you do.

DOWNTOWN CHOPPER CHECKPOINT

This Sparrow is Downtown on the first building you drive onto in the "G-Spotlight" mission. Enter it to begin the Downtown Chopper Checkpoint. This challenge takes you low—along the street of the Downtown area, under the V.A.J Finance building, and through the building you jump through in the "G-Spotlight" mission. There are 28 checkpoints—most are located just above the narrow streets, in between buildings. It may be difficult to keep your blades off buildings and your helicopter in good enough condition to complete the challenge. Luckily, you are only racing against your own best time, so take it easy, learn the route, and then try to improve your skills the next time through.

Shooting Range

Return to the Downtown Ammu-Nation after completing "The Shootist" mission to compete in a shooting competition that takes place in the back of the store.

Hit as many targets as you can in the time limit. When you run out of time or ammunition, the round is over. To exit the round, press the Square Button. If you leave the shooting range during the competition, you will fail the mission. Use the same tactics used to beat "The Shootist" mission—it's the exact same challenge. You will receive $500 each time you pass this mission.

FAST LOAD
Score higher than 45 to unlock the Fast Load ability. This takes away the loading animation and speeds up firing between magazines. The Rocket Launcher is greatly improved by Fast Load.

SHOOTING RANGE COMP

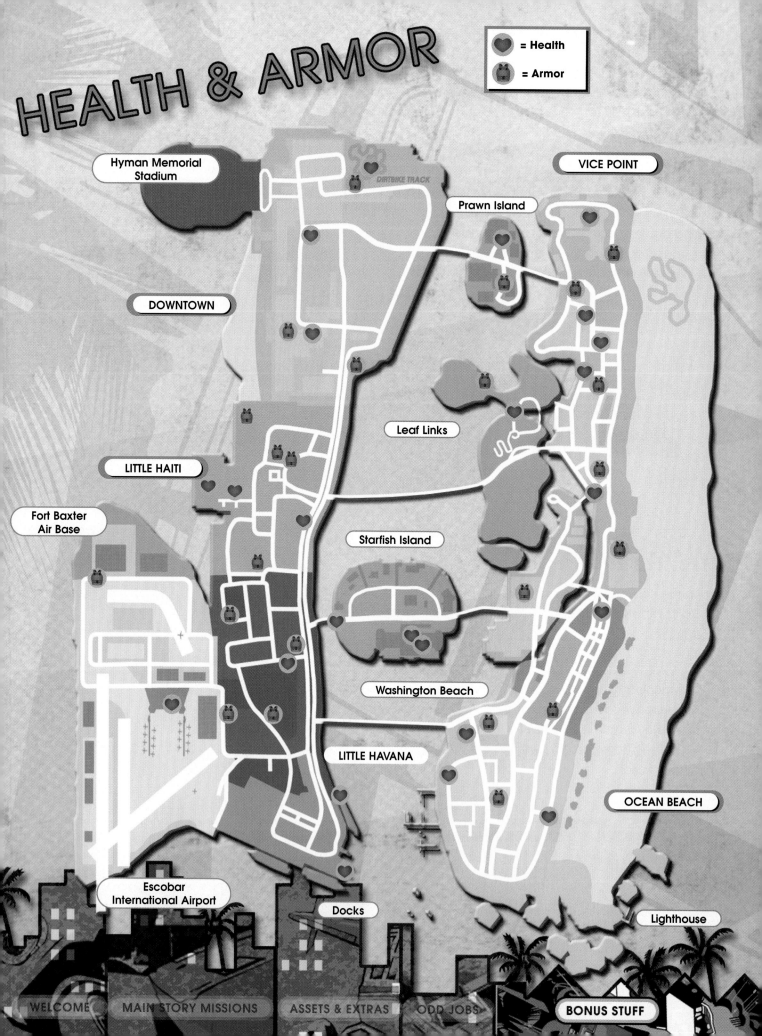

HEALTH & ARMOR

♥ = Health

▣ = Armor

Hyman Memorial Stadium

VICE POINT

DIRTBIKE TRACK

Prawn Island

DOWNTOWN

Leaf Links

LITTLE HAITI

Fort Baxter Air Base

Starfish Island

Washington Beach

LITTLE HAVANA

OCEAN BEACH

Escobar International Airport

Docks

Lighthouse

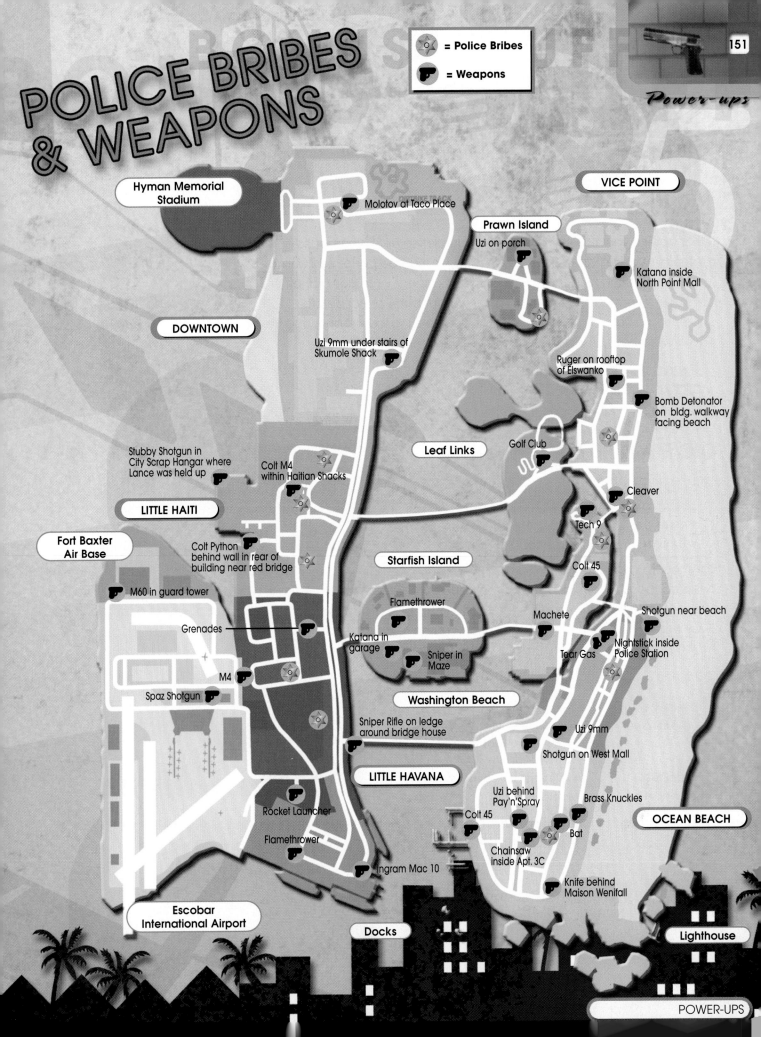

RAMPAGES

This chapter is your ticket to finding and completing all 35 Rampages hidden throughout Vice City. These challenges must be performed during specific missions; in fact, the skull icon will not appear while doing another job. Make sure you're at full health and have full body armor before attempting a Rampage. You earn $50 for completing the first one, and the payoff increases in $50 increments with each successive Rampage.

Map Icons
Square icons represent locations on the ground level. Triangle icons identify the ones above Tommy's head. These higher locations may require stair climbing, roof jumping, motorcycle jumps, or flight via helicopter or plane to reach them.

The Beach

OCEAN BEACH 💀

DISTRICT:	Viceport/Ocean Beach
LOCATION:	On dilapidated dock in the water.
RAMPAGE:	Destroy 10 vehicles in 2 minutes.
WEAPON:	Rocket Launcher

Stand on the stairs where the Rampage is found and destroy the boats as they appear. Lines of boats appear to the northeast and in another position due east. Once you've destroyed a boat in one location (and if you don't see another), turn and look toward the second spawn location. The boats appear at an equal distance away from you in both locations, so once you have your weapon set, you need only move your weapon to the left and right to maintain your sight on the boats. Fire as often as you like, the shells are unlimited.

DISTRICT:	Ocean Beach
LOCATION:	In bushes near the water to the south, where the walkway to the lighthouse branches from the street.
RAMPAGE:	Kill 30 gang members in 2 minutes.
WEAPON:	Molotov Cocktails

Throw Molotovs at the groups of denim-clad gang member wannabes walking along the lighthouse trail—they're wearing white T-shirts. Avoid getting too close to the groups or you'll burn yourself with short lobs.

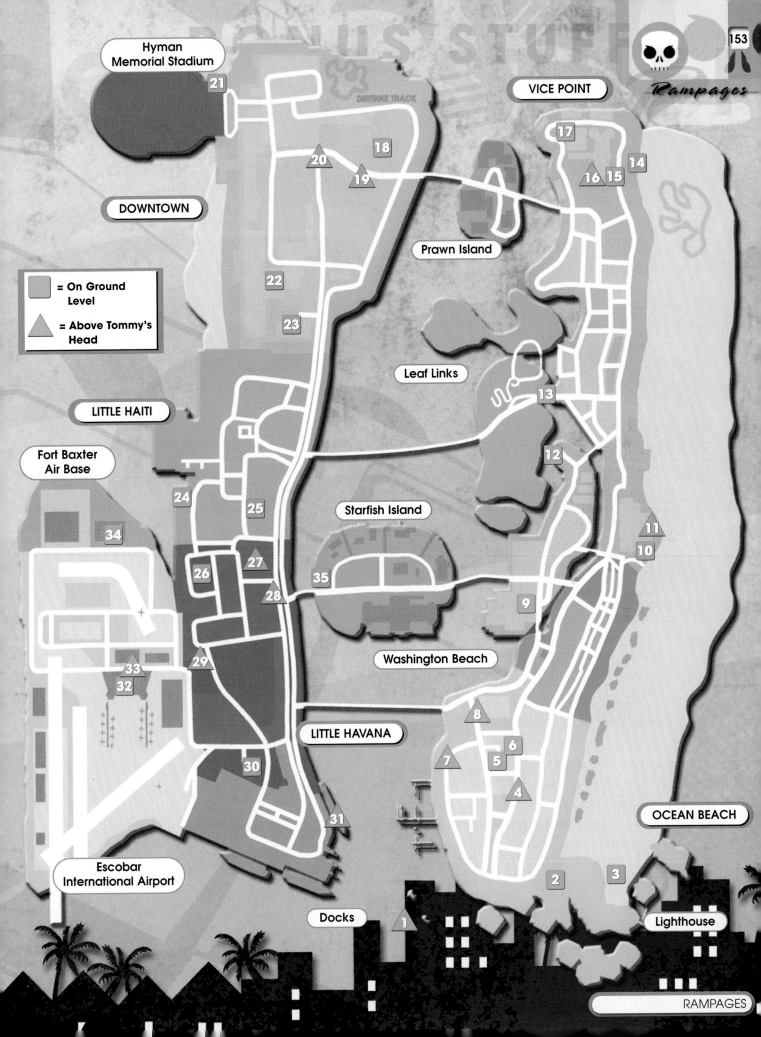

Rampages

Hyman Memorial Stadium

21

DIRTBIKE TRACK

VICE POINT

17

18

20

14

19

16 15

DOWNTOWN

Prawn Island

13

= On Ground Level

= Above Tommy's Head

Leaf Links

12

LITTLE HAITI

Fort Baxter Air Base

24

11

34

10

25

Starfish Island

26

27

35

9

28

Washington Beach

29

8

LITTLE HAVANA

7

6

33

5

32

4

30

31

OCEAN BEACH

2

3

Escobar International Airport

Docks

1

Lighthouse

3

DISTRICT:	Ocean Beach
LOCATION:	On the beach near the shoreline, just north of the lighthouse.
RAMPAGE:	Run over and kill 30 gang members in 2 minutes.
WEAPON:	Vehicle of your choice

It's a good idea to drive a vehicle up to this Rampage location so you don't waste time searching for a car to jack while the clock is ticking away. However, if you didn't bring a vehicle, there is just enough time to run to the street to the west, jack a car, and begin plowing down Diaz's boys that gather along the lighthouse trail.

4

DISTRICT:	Ocean Beach
LOCATION:	On the top corner of the two-story building connected to the vine-covered carpark.
RAMPAGE:	Kill 25 gang members in 2 minutes.
WEAPON:	Vehicle of your choice

Stand on the very edge of the roof, then use the R1 Button to enter the scope mode and the Square and X Buttons to zoom in and out. Look up and down the sidewalks below and start capping all the gang members wearing white T-shirts. Standing on the edge of the rooftop allows you to see and shoot the gang members standing on the sidewalk directly below you.

5

DISTRICT:	Ocean Beach
LOCATION:	Near the fence and under a palm tree in the backyard of a congested neighborhood.
RAMPAGE:	Kill 10 gang members in 2 minutes.
WEAPON:	Katana

Run out to the closest street, then stand in the middle of a gang and start swinging. Keep moving to avoid the gang's bullets. Running by them while swinging is much better than standing and picking a fight with one gang member at a time. If you get too close to the opponent, Tommy fights with his arms and legs instead of the Katana.

6

DISTRICT:	Ocean Beach
LOCATION:	Behind the concrete fence of the east pink apartment tower (the OakDale Tolet).
RAMPAGE:	Kill 20 gang members in 2 minutes.
WEAPON:	Chainsaw

Run out onto the street and search for the groups of gang members. The best attack strategy is to run through the gang gatherings while holding down the Circle Button; this ensures the chainsaw cuts anyone it touches. You run slowly while this weapon is equipped and there's no way to put it away during this challenge, so keep moving to avoid the gang's bullets—no matter how slow you may be running. Run back and forth on the street and you'll find plenty of gang members in huddles.

DISTRICT:	Ocean Beach
LOCATION:	On the east side of the Ocean View Medical R&D building.
RAMPAGE:	Kill 25 gang members in 2 minutes.
WEAPON:	M4

Remain on the grassy ledge where you find the Rampage and approach the edge overlooking the street. Use the R1 Button to activate the first-person aiming view, then begin picking off the Haitians (they're wearing blue and white clothing). When the area is clear, or you cannot hit the Haitians on the sidewalk directly below you, jump down and start spraying the masses.

DISTRICT:	Ocean Beach
LOCATION:	Near Unique Stunt jump on the rooftop of the Washington Mall.
RAMPAGE:	Kill 25 gang members in 2 minutes.
WEAPON:	Chromed Shotgun

Jump over the ledge of the mall's rooftop parking lot and into the pond on the ground floor of the mall. This is a great place to do your deadly work. Gang members are all around and not many of them make it over the lip of the pond. Crouch down and start blowing away all the thugs. When you've exhausted the area of gang members, head up the escalator and clear the second floor of the mall rats. If you run out of targets again, head back downstairs and more gang members will show up.

WASHINGTON BEACH

DISTRICT:	Washington Beach
LOCATION:	Behind the orange half wall of the pool house at Hotel Foyet, near Bunch of Tools.
RAMPAGE:	Kill 25 gang members in 2 minutes.
WEAPON:	MP5

Head east toward the large street near Bunch of Tools, then crouch and shoot into the mob of gang members. Get up and move around to find more groups of thugs. Be sure to shoot the gang members that are shooting at you before concentrating your attack on the less threatening variety. Keep a steady stream of bullets sweeping through the gang by using the L2-R2 targeting sweep.

DISTRICT:	Washington Beach
LOCATION:	In the bushes behind the Standing Vice Point Hotel, on the same side of the building as the pool and Rampage #11.
RAMPAGE:	Kill 30 gang members in 2 minutes.
WEAPON:	Spaz 12 Shotgun

After passing through the Rampage icon, turn and head south around the building, then start targeting the gang members from behind the half wall along the beach walkway. Head west toward the main street when you've exhausted the gang supply to cause some more mayhem there. With the Spaz Shotgun, no one will likely get near you, so this mission should be accomplished quickly.

VICE POINT

DISTRICT:	Vice Point
LOCATION:	Behind hotel in the middle of the island, on top of the highest diving board.
RAMPAGE:	Kill 30 gang members in 2 minutes.
WEAPON:	Spaz 12 Shotgun

Remain on the diving board and look down toward the hotel for the gang members with the white T-shirts. Use the R1 Button to enter the scope view and press the Square and X Buttons to zoom in and out as you pick them off one by one.

DISTRICT:	Vice Point
LOCATION:	On the grass at the end of the cul-de-sac.
RAMPAGE:	Drive-by and waste 35 gang members in 2 minutes.
WEAPON:	Ingram Mac 10

Drive a durable vehicle to this Rampage location. This drive-by mission isn't too terribly difficult—there are plenty of Rising Sun T-shirts to shoot on the roundabout. When the gangs thin out, take to the nearby streets and search for more targets. Your biggest challenge will be trying not to alert the police too early in the challenge. If they show up when you're one-third of the way through, you'll be able to mow them down and continue on your primary targets. Your Wanted Level goes back down when you've completed the mission.

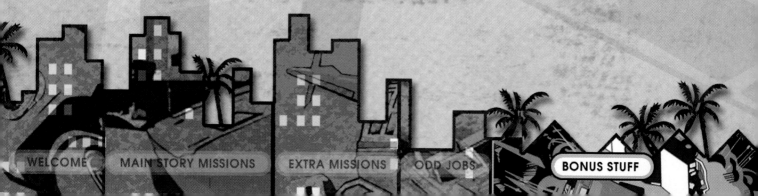

DISTRICT:	Vice Point
LOCATION:	On the dock near the bridge behind Mercedes' house.
RAMPAGE:	Kill 20 gang members in 2 minutes.
WEAPON:	Chainsaw

13

Run back up the dock (as fast as you can with the heavy chainsaw), then climb the grassy knoll and enter the street near the bridge. Look for the first group of gang members, then hold down the Circle Button and let 'er rip. Try to keep moving to avoid their attacks. Keep your thumb on the Circle Button to avoid the need to press it twice when someone is on the ground at your feet—the lengthy chainsaw massacre move could cost you your life because you're so vulnerable when standing still.

DISTRICT:	Vice Point
LOCATION:	On North Beach, north of the Dirtbike track next to the seawall.
RAMPAGE:	Kill 25 gang members in 2 minutes.
WEAPON:	Python

14

Head for the street in front of North Point Mall and start shooting the many gang members. The quickest way to knock them off and avoid conflict is to press the R1 Button to target, hold the Circle Button to fire, and press the L2 or R2 Button after each hit to target and shoot the next closest gang member. It's not even necessary to press the Circle Button to fire until you release the R1 Button to run toward the next group of gang members.

DISTRICT:	Vice Point
LOCATION:	On the grass beside the southeast entrance to North Point Mall.
RAMPAGE:	Kill 35 gang members in 2 minutes.
WEAPON:	M4

15

Remain in the Rampage location area and just start mowing down the gang members—there are plenty in this area. Use the aiming feature on your weapon—it helps keep you out of fistfights when the thugs get close.

DISTRICT:	Vice Point
LOCATION:	Inside the North Point Mall, in a planter near the Vinyl Countdown (a spoof on Europe's song).
RAMPAGE:	Kill 35 gang members in 2 minutes.
WEAPON:	Rocket Launcher

16

Use the Rocket Launcher to eliminate groups of gang members around the mall. Once the top floor seems clear, head downstairs and continue your rampage. Keeping your distance from gang members is key to completing this mission.

17		
DISTRICT:	Vice Point	
LOCATION:	Behind a building near the oar park.	
RAMPAGE:	Drive-by and waste 30 gang members in 2 minutes.	
WEAPON:	Uzi and the vehicle of your choice	

Jack any vehicle in the street, then drive around the immediate area and spray the sidewalk-cruisin' gang members. If they approach your door, shoot 'em!

The Mainland

DOWNTOWN

18		
DISTRICT:	Downtown	
LOCATION:	In the V.A.J building's center courtyard, near a door behind the funky sculpture.	
RAMPAGE:	Kill 30 gang members in 2 minutes.	
WEAPON:	Minigun	

As soon as you grab the Rampage, sprint toward the street to the north and unload on all the gang members. This is a very powerful weapon, so avoid standing anywhere close to cars that may get caught in your spray of bullets—the explosion will cause major hurt. The toughest part of this mission is keeping your head. Shooting a cop attracts more heat and makes the mission even tougher. However, the Wanted Level goes away upon completion of the mission. Keep turning from left to right to make sure gang members aren't sneaking up on you. You really don't need a fistfight, as it invites the others you've enraged to attack. This battle is loads of fun!

19		
DISTRICT:	Downtown	
LOCATION:	On the stairs of the large, white apartment buildings south of the V.A.J finance building.	
RAMPAGE:	Kill 40 gang members in 2 minutes.	
WEAPON:	Molotov Cocktails	

Simply run out to the nearest street and start chucking bottles of gasoline into the crowd. Run up and down the street to find more groups of gang members. Remember, the throw button is analog, so the longer and harder you press it, the farther the toss. Don't drop the Molotov too close to where you're standing or *you'll* be the one that needs a doctor!

20

DISTRICT:	Downtown
LOCATION:	On a large set of stairs across from Ammu-Nation (used for missions and a Unique Stunt Jump).
RAMPAGE:	Kill 25 gang members in 2 minutes.
WEAPON:	Python

Jump down from the stairs, then run around the street in front of Ammu-Nation popping all the gang members you see. Implement the targeting tactics used in previous Rampages.

21

DISTRICT:	Downtown
LOCATION:	To the right of the stadium, near the helipad docks.
RAMPAGE:	Kill 30 gang members in 2 minutes.
WEAPON:	Flame-thrower

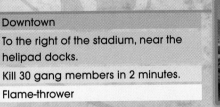

Waste the groups that gather near the Rampage. After toasting all the gang members in this area, head toward the stadium stairs to attack the mobs that congregate against the wall below the stairs. Return to the Rampage location and you'll find more gang members. Continue these rounds to char 30 thugs in less than two minutes.

22

DISTRICT:	Downtown
LOCATION:	In an alley behind the buildings beside the Pizza Restaurant.
RAMPAGE:	Drive-by and waste 35 gang members in 2 minutes.
WEAPON:	Ingram Mac 10

Run out into the street in front of the Pizza place, grab a car (unless you have one already), and drive down the local streets. Finding enough gang members to plug will be no problem, just don't let them yank you out of your vehicle!

23

DISTRICT:	Downtown
LOCATION:	Behind the Moist Palms Hotel.
RAMPAGE:	Kill 30 gang members in 2 minutes.
WEAPON:	M60

Head for the closest street, then use the R1 Button to access the weapon's sight mode and shoot into the crowd of bikers. When the ambulance arrives, avoid shooting the paramedics. These guys heal the fallen gang members, giving you another chance to kill the same victims, and improving your hit count.

LITTLE HAITI

24	

DISTRICT:	Little Haiti
LOCATION:	Behind a scummy one-story building (Vice City Port Authority bldg.) on the cobbled area near the water and the small red bridge.
RAMPAGE:	Kill 35 gang members in 2 minutes.
WEAPON:	Spaz 12 Shotgun

Run into the heart of Little Haiti and waste all the Haitian gang members (they wear all sorts of colors, but mostly blue and white). There are plenty of targets, so this Rampage should go off without a hitch.

25

DISTRICT:	Little Haiti
LOCATION:	In an alley behind the buildings beside the Pizza Restaurant.
RAMPAGE:	Kill 30 gang members in 2 minutes.
WEAPON:	Tec9

Head out to the nearest street where you'll find hordes of Haitians (blue and white clothing). Crouch and shoot into the crowds. When shooting the gang members, sporadically let up on the fire button, and then press it again to improve the accuracy of the shots. The longer you hold down on the fire button, the less accurate your aim becomes. Letting up on the button and then pressing it again lets loose the better-aimed bullets. Wasting 35 thugs is a cinch with this weapon.

LITTLE HAVANA

26

DISTRICT:	Little Havana
LOCATION:	In the fenced-in basketball court.
RAMPAGE:	Kill 25 gang members in 2 minutes.
WEAPON:	Chromed Shotgun

Head for the streets and press the R1 Button to target the gang members. Hold down on R1 and the Circle Button while switching targets and firing every time you press the L2 or R2 Button. The Spaz has an incredible range and you can practically remain in one place while panning around and blasting victims. Crouch down for better accuracy and improved odds of missing enemy bullets. If you shoot a distant target, make sure to check on him a little later—he may have gotten back up for more.

DISTRICT:	Little Havana
LOCATION:	In the corner of a loading bay behind the VC Bank (tall blue-and-white building), near red-roofed buildings.
RAMPAGE:	Kill 20 gang members in 2 minutes.
WEAPON:	Katana

Grab the Rampage and hit the nearest street. There are loads of Cubans in the area, so finding enough to run through is not the problem—in fact, their ubiquity is the problem. Once you attack a group of gang members, you've just thrown the proverbial rock at the hornet's nest. Keep moving! You can run with the Katana in hand. Hold the Circle Button to put the Katana in a permanent ready position. Release the Circle Button and Tommy will bring the blade down. This Rampage is difficult—slashing an opponent down to the ground does not always mean he is dead. Only decapitating or running through brings an opponent down with one hit. Avoid getting caught up in large groups, and don't stand too close to anyone. You have a sword, so use it!

DISTRICT:	Little Havana
LOCATION:	On top of the lower rooftop of the West Haven Community Healthcare Center.
RAMPAGE:	Gun down 20 gang members in 2 minutes.
WEAPON:	Sniper Rifle

28

This is one of the tougher Rampage challenges. Two minutes is not much time to kill the required number of gang members this time. Remain on the rooftop as long as possible (until you've wasted all the gang members you can see) to avoid police attention, then jump down and patrol the sidewalk to find more targets. Continue to shoot gang members from a distance to avoid up-close confrontation. Watch the bridge across the road—gang members approach from there. Allow the paramedics to heal the dead so you'll have more targets.

DISTRICT:	Little Havana
LOCATION:	On the rooftop of the building with the red awning (this is also a Hidden Package location).
RAMPAGE:	Kill 20 gang members in 2 minutes.
WEAPON:	Ruger

29

Stay on the rooftop where you find the Rampage and approach the edge of the roof overlooking the street below. Press the R1 Button and take aim at the many Haitians on the sidewalks below. There's no need to hop down to ground level and search for possible victims; plenty of gang members appear while at your perch on the rooftop.

VICEPORT 💀

DISTRICT:	Escobar International
LOCATION:	Behind Hooker Inn, among the bushes.
RAMPAGE:	Kill 35 gang members in 2 minutes.
WEAPON:	Grenades

Run into the street in front of the Hooker Inn and begin lobbing grenades into the mobs of gang members. If you're having trouble putting just the right amount of strength into the toss, try running up to the crowd, tapping on the Circle Button to drop a grenade, and then quickly running away. You can sprint at full speed when holding grenades, and there's enough time to escape the concussion after dropping a bomb.

31

DISTRICT:	Viceport/The Docks
LOCATION:	On the east ship at the docks. The Rampage is behind the thick white mast in the middle of the ship.
RAMPAGE:	Destroy 15 vehicles in 2 minutes.
WEAPON:	Rocket Launcher

Approach the closest boarding ramp, but remain on the ship (this makes it more difficult for the angry mobs to reach you). From this vantage point, shoot the vehicles that come and go from the docks. Shoot into crowds to bring ambulances and police, then destroy their vehicles, too.

ESCOBAR INTERNATIONAL 💀

32

DISTRICT:	Escobar International
LOCATION:	On the ground floor of the airport, behind the check-in desks (walk along the windowed wall).
RAMPAGE:	Kill 25 gang members in 2 minutes.
WEAPON:	Spaz 12 Shotgun

Run into the main terminal and waste the Haitians, then head for the other side of the terminal—there aren't enough gang members to stay in one area. If you clear the lower floor, head up the escalators to find groups of Haitians gathered around the railings overlooking the first floor. Luckily, there's no police interference, because they're so slow to arrive and actually enter the terminal.

DISTRICT:	Escobar International
LOCATION:	On the rooftop of the of the Escobar International Terminal.
RAMPAGE:	Destroy 15 vehicles in 2 minutes.
WEAPON:	Rocket Launcher

33

Remain on the rooftop of the Terminal and begin firing shells at traffic. Shoot crowds of people so the police and ambulances arrive (they bring more vehicles to the airport). When the traffic ceases, head across the rooftop toward the busy intersection to the east to destroy cabs and other travelers.

DISTRICT:	Escobar International
LOCATION:	Behind some bushes near the northernmost road on the airport peninsula, east of Fort Baxter.
RAMPAGE:	Destroy 20 vehicles in 2 minutes..
WEAPON:	Minigun

34

The tough thing about this mission is that the closest road is the only road—since there's not enough time to lug your heavy weapon to another one. Make sure you perform this mission in the daytime when there are plenty of vehicles traveling on this road. The only way to get enough vehicles to arrive during the time allotted is to shoot the people around and start attacking ambulances and police cars. Moving a little further up and down the street also helps generate traffic.

STARFISH ISLAND 💀

DISTRICT:	Starfish Island
LOCATION:	In the driveway of the westernmost house on Starfish Island, north of the bridge.
RAMPAGE:	Run over and kill 35 gang members in 2 minutes.
WEAPON:	Vehicle of your choice

35

Walk over the hedges of this house to get access the Rampage. Head into the street and jack a car, or enter the one you arrived in, and begin running over the many Haitians on the sidewalks. The faster you drive, the more likely your victims will die on impact; otherwise, you may need to back over them when they get back up.

UNIQUE STUNT JUMPS

Find the following location numbers on the Unique Stunt Jump map (see next page). Speed is the key to all unique jumps—the Unique Stunt is awarded only when the aerial cinematic is triggered. Use high-end sports cars to conquer these jumps. When space is limited to build up speed before the jump, use the PCJ 600.

Map Icons

Square icons represent locations on the ground level. Triangle icons identify the ones above Tommy's head.

The Mainland

DOWNTOWN

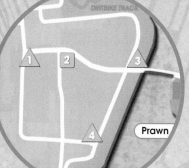

1 Jump from the ramp on top of the hospital to the roof of the Secondhand Circuitry building across the street. (This jump is performed in the "G-Spotlight" mission.)

2 Jump the large set of stairs and land on top of the Ammu-Nation building. (This jump is performed in the "Hog Tied" mission.)

3 Last jump from high-rise to spotlight rooftop. (This jump is performed in the "G-Spotlight" mission.)

4 Smash through the glass in a PCJ 600 and land in the hollow area in the building across the street. (This jump is performed in the "G-Spotlight" mission.)

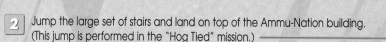
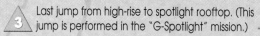

LITTLE HAITI

5 Use alley ramp to jump storage containers, through a Police Bribe and onto Riverside Pavillion rooftop where you can access a helicopter challenge.

6 Jump the wooden ramp on the crate in the grassy alley, then soar above the old school bus and over the adjacent house.

7 Jump the wooden ramp through the Police Bribe and fly over the drainage channel.

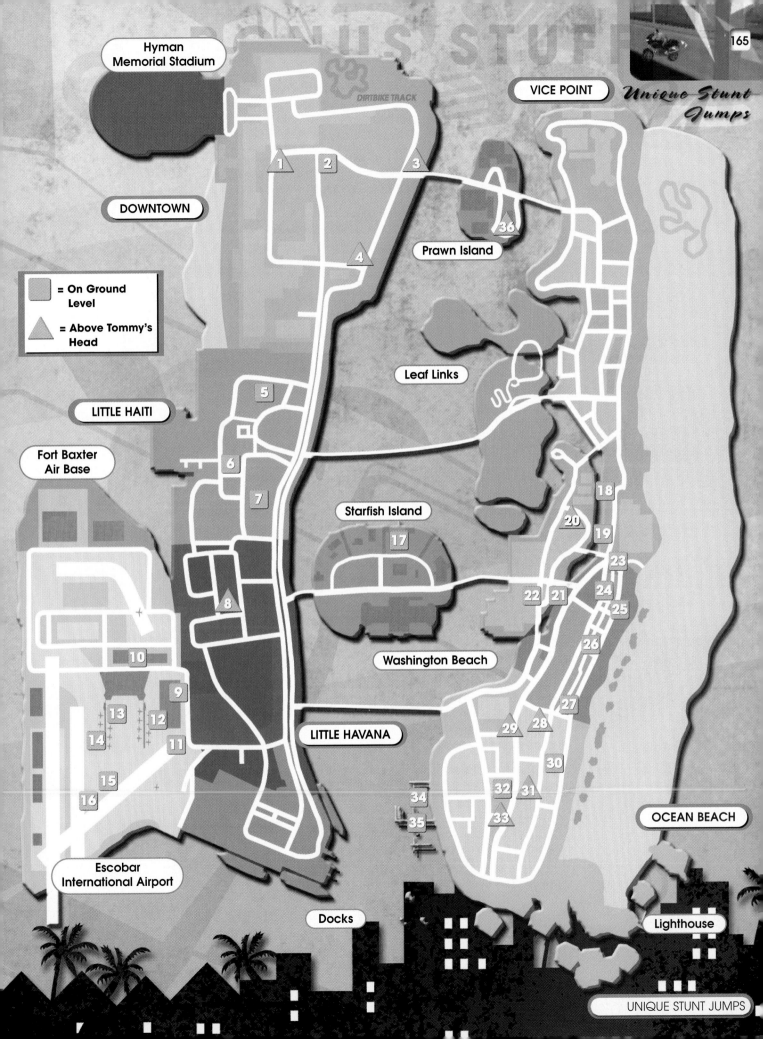

Hyman Memorial Stadium

DIRTBIKE TRACK

VICE POINT

Unique Stunt Jumps

DOWNTOWN

1 2 3

36

Prawn Island

4

= On Ground Level

= Above Tommy's Head

Leaf Links

LITTLE HAITI

Fort Baxter Air Base

5

6

7

Starfish Island

18

20

19

17

23

22 21

24

25

26

Washington Beach

8

10

9

13 12

14 11

15

16

27

29 28

30

LITTLE HAVANA

32 31

34

33

35

Escobar International Airport

OCEAN BEACH

Docks

Lighthouse

LITTLE HAVANA

Use the rooftop slope on top of Calle 8 Cafeteria to jump the street and land on the roof of the 1-HR Photo store. You'll have to build up speed using ramps and slopes, starting a few rooftops south of the first ramp.

ESCOBAR INTERNATIONAL AIRPORT

Escobar International Airport

9 Use the mobile stairs to jump the fence and land in the parking lot across the street, or on the Vice City Transport Police building.

10 Use the large Vice Surf 3D billboard as a ramp to reach the top of the airport terminal.

11 Use the lift ramp to jump over the fence and land in street beyond.

12 Use the mobile stairs to jump over the easternmost loading bridge, heading west.

13 Use the mobile stairs to jump over the westernmost loaden bridge, heading west.

14 Use mobile stairs to jump over the westernmost loading bridge, heading east.

15 On the opposite side of jump location #17, use the yellow runway marker to jump the radar building.

16 Use mobile stairs next to the red radar building to jump as high as you can.

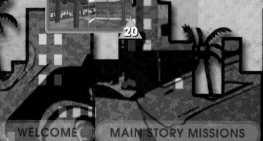

Starfish Island

Starfish Island

17 There are some steps on the south side of the brown stucco house on the northern coast of the island. Back up into the yard to the west (you'll see a small gate open next to the garage) and use this area to build up enough speed to fly into the yard and up the steps. Jump over the hedges and into the neighbors' yard to the east.

The Beach

VICE POINT

18 On the south side of The Malibu, find the cement ramp near the channel. Get a running start from the parking lot across the street, fly up the ramp, and clear the channel (heading west).

19 There's another cement ramp that's south of The Malibu and jump #18, along the same grassy strip of land along the channel. It's near the bridge to the peninsula. Hit the ramp, heading south, and jump over the bridge.

20 On the top level of the building under construction (near Hidden Package #20) is a girder that angles upward and angles off at a northward incline. Use the PCJ 600 to speed along this long girder and complete the Unique Stunt.

Unique Stunt Jumps

WASHINGTON BEACH

21 Start on the west side of the channel and jump the dirt pile south of the small bridge that leads across the water. Back all the way up to the Starfish Island bridge to build up enough speed to hit the dirt pile, then sail over the channel and land on the east island.

22 When jumping across the channel from jump #21, you pass over jump #22; it's the cement ramp south of the bridge to Starfish Island, on the grassy path along the channel. Use it to jump across the channel and over the dirt mound that is jump #21.

23 At the first jump in PCJ Playground. Jump the wooden ramp over the rooftop of the building on the corner, then jump over the ramp on the rooftop and land on top of the second building to the south.

24 Further north, in the same alley as jump #26, is another similar set of metal stairs against a building on the right. Jump across the street and over or on top of the building to the north in the next alley. This is the same set of stairs used as a vantage point when you protected Diaz in the "Guardian Angels" mission.

25 This stairway jump is across the ally from jump #24; the stairs Lance was standing on in the "Guardian Angels" mission. Approach this jump from the east. Build up speed from the beach wall and drive west, then steer between the telephone pole and the corner of the building and go up the stairs on west side of the building. Jump over the building to the west, over the street, and land in the grass near the Police Station.

26 Jump the large set of metal stairs against the building in the alley. Sail across the street heading north, and land on the building across the street.

27 North of jump #28 and in the same alleyway. Jump a similar stack of pallets, but heading south this time. Jump across the street and land on the building or just far enough into the alley to trigger the jump animation.

OCEAN BEACH

28 Use the rooftop vents to jump from the top of the two-story white building on the corner, then fly over the street and land on top of the building to the east.

29 Jump from the ramp close to the shotgun power-up on the rooftop parking lot of Washington Mall. Fly across the street, heading east, and land on the Beach Scooter store.

30 Jump the stack of two pallets in the alley and land on the rooftop of the building to the north, on the left side of the alley.

31 Jump from the ramp of the Cone Crazy (carpark) rooftop, heading south, and land on the rooftop of the Collar & Cuffs building across the street.

32 Use the stairs beneath the white building on stilts to jump south, clear across adjacent building across the next street, and land on the apartments with pink rooftop. Use a bike and back all the way down the alley to the north to gain speed.

33 Continue your steam from the previous jump (#32), and hit the ramp on the pink rooftop. Jump the street, still heading south, and land on the rooftop of the next building. (Even if you don't make it all the way to the roof, sufficient distance will complete the challenge.)

34 Use the PCJ 600 to jump from the north pier (near the Colonel's yacht) to the south pier (jump #35).

35 Launch from the pier used in jump #34, then continue racing over the following wooden ramp to reach the southernmost pier.

Prawn Island

36 Use a PCJ 600 to jump the ramp on the roof of the southernmost corner building—you'll soar over the film studio wall and land in the studio's back lot. Use sloped stairs of the northern building behind it to access the correct ramp's rooftop.

Prawn Island

HIDDEN PACKAGES

Rewards

The following list details how many packages are needed to unlock weapons and vehicles, and where they can be found once unlocked. Get the reward locations upstairs in your hotel room and connecting hallways of the Ocean View Hotel. You can also find them along the eastern outside wall in front of the maze at your mansion (after acquiring it from Diaz) on Starfish Island. The Rhino and the final big prize are created at Fort Baxter Air Base.

Packages	Reward	Reward Location
10	Body Armor	Ocean View Hotel & Starfish Island Mansion
20	Chainsaw	Ocean View Hotel & Starfish Island Mansion
30	Python	Ocean View Hotel & Starfish Island Mansion
40	Flame-thrower	Ocean View Hotel & Starfish Island Mansion
50	Laser Scope Sniper Rifle	Ocean View Hotel & Starfish Island Mansion
60	Minigun	Ocean View Hotel & Starfish Island Mansion
70	Rocket Launcher	Ocean View Hotel & Starfish Island Mansion
80	Sea Sparrow	Starfish Island Mansion's Helipad
90	Rhino	Fort Baxter Air Base
100	Ultimate Secret Vehicle	Fort Baxter Air Base

Locations

This section details every Hidden Package location; the numbers correspond to the icon on our Hidden Packages map. Square icons represent packages on the ground level and Triangle icons identify the ones above Tommy's head. These higher packages may require stair climbing, roof jumping, motorcycle jumps, or flight via helicopter or plane.

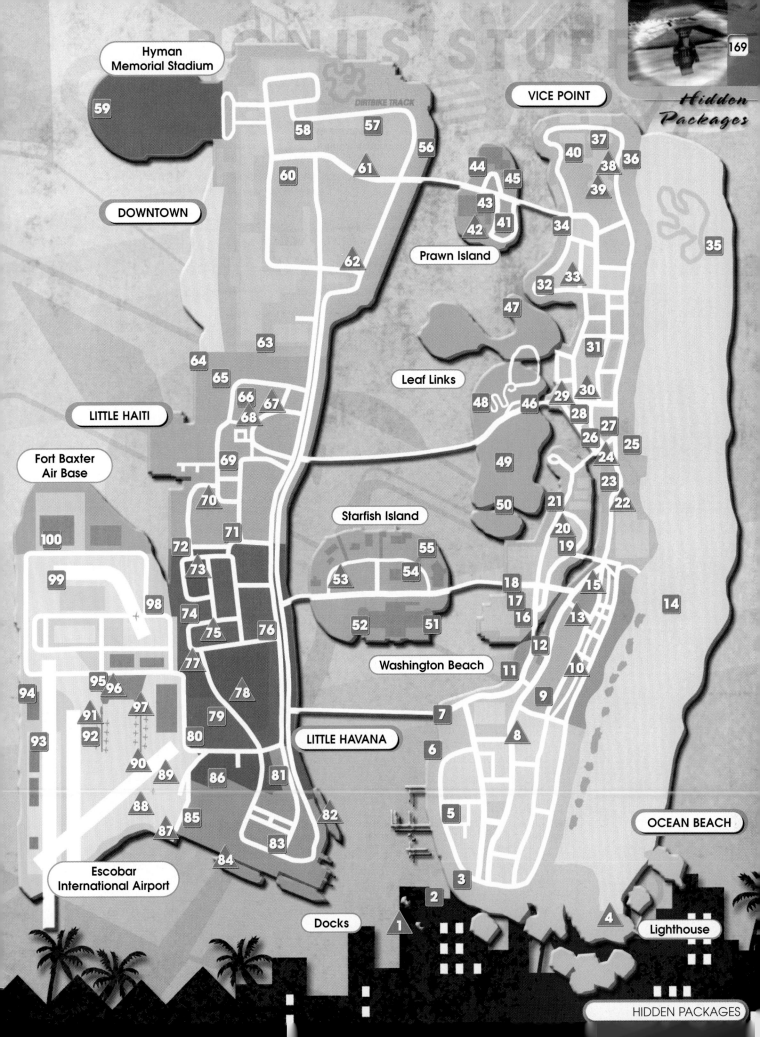

Hyman Memorial Stadium

VICE POINT

Hidden Packages

DOWNTOWN

Prawn Island

Leaf Links

LITTLE HAITI

Fort Baxter Air Base

Starfish Island

Washington Beach

LITTLE HAVANA

Escobar International Airport

OCEAN BEACH

Docks

Lighthouse

The Beach

OCEAN BEACH

1 On desecrated wooden hut platform in the water.

2 On rocks near wooden huts in the water.

3 Next to the steps of the southernmost house on the island.

4 On the steps of the lighthouse.

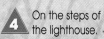

5 In a corner in the underground carpark at the marina (where you pick up the Colonel's missions).

6 On a ledge near the water, behind the west Ocean View Medical Foundation Research and Development building.

7 On a narrow walkway under the South Bridge, leading to the mainland.

8 On top of the one-story building across from the small Washington Mall.

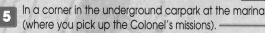

WASHINGTON BEACH

9 Near the fenced-in swimming pool of the large pink apartment building, next to the body armor.

10 On top of the two-story building connected to the DBP Security building.

11 On back porch overlooking water of your save house, across from Rosenberg's office.

12 On the ground near the water's edge, up against the small road bridge.

13 On top of the tall blue-and-white building with the old white wooden fence (use a helicopter to reach).

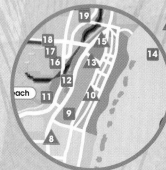

14 On the steps of a lifeguard hut on the beach.

15 In upstairs office of the Vice City Police Department.

16 In a corner of a purple-and-white one-story building with peach trim. The package is facing a small mote in front of the building.

17 In the multi-colored open showers near the pool on the hotel grounds, near the bridge to Starfish Island.

18 On the ground underneath the bridge leading to Starfish Island.

VICE POINT

19 In small alley behind SpandEX delivery firm.

20 At the end of the I-beam that juts out from the third floor of the building under construction.

21 On a dock facing Golf Island.

22 Near the pool on top of building that's catty-corner from The Malibu.

23 In a corner, behind the gates of The Malibu.

24 On the top (pool area) of the building where Candy and the Congressman were partying in the "Martha's Mugshot" mission.

25 Behind WK Chariot Hotel.

26 Inside the Pizza Restaurant.

27 On the ground behind the stairs of the corner apartment building, next to the Pizza Restaurant.

28 Inside Jewelry shop, behind the counter.

29 Near back exit of Mercedes' house.

30 On the second rooftop where you pursue the thug in "The Chase" mission.

31 In backyard, in the corner of a fence, east of the north Pay 'n' Spray.

32 Inside the walled-in corner of hairpin turn.

33 On top of the highest diving board at the pool behind the hotel.

34 On the waterfront sidewalk, up against the south side of the bridge leading to the film studio island.

35 Behind Jocksport sign on beach, next to RC Bandit track.

36 Behind apartment building to the east of the North Point Mall.

37 In the nook between north entrances, outside the North Point Mall.

38 Upstairs in the North Point Mall, on the east side, in front of a store with sale signs.

39 Upstairs in the North Point Mall, inside a store called "Gash."

40 On ground level of large multi-story car park near the North Point Mall.

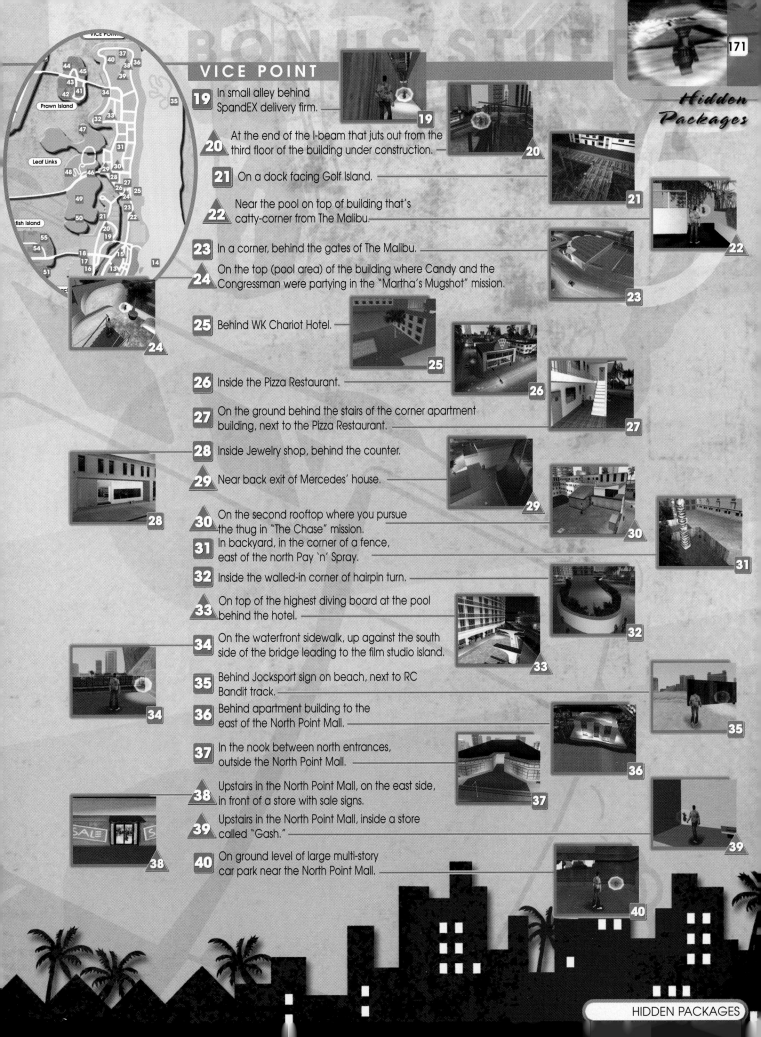

Prawn Island

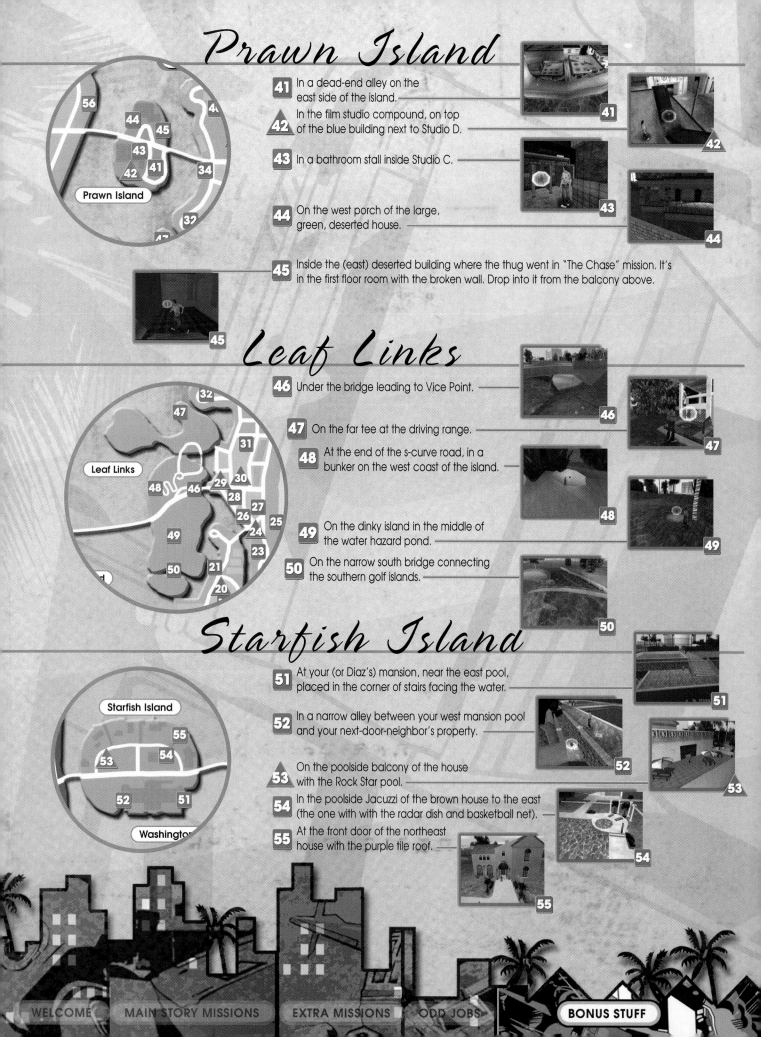

41 In a dead-end alley on the east side of the island.

42 In the film studio compound, on top of the blue building next to Studio D.

43 In a bathroom stall inside Studio C.

44 On the west porch of the large, green, deserted house.

45 Inside the (east) deserted building where the thug went in "The Chase" mission. It's in the first floor room with the broken wall. Drop into it from the balcony above.

Leaf Links

46 Under the bridge leading to Vice Point.

47 On the far tee at the driving range.

48 At the end of the s-curve road, in a bunker on the west coast of the island.

49 On the dinky island in the middle of the water hazard pond.

50 On the narrow south bridge connecting the southern golf islands.

Starfish Island

51 At your (or Diaz's) mansion, near the east pool, placed in the corner of stairs facing the water.

52 In a narrow alley between your west mansion pool and your next-door-neighbor's property.

53 On the poolside balcony of the house with the Rock Star pool.

54 In the poolside Jacuzzi of the brown house to the east (the one with with the radar dish and basketball net).

55 At the front door of the northeast house with the purple tile roof.

The Mainland

DOWNTOWN

56 Behind the last building you jump from in the "G-Spotlight" mission, in a nook facing the water.

57 In the sculpture of the V.A.J finance building.

58 Behind the Mars Café (where Love First's Psycho attacked). Use the save house alley to reach the package.

59 In the parking lot behind the stadium (west side).

60 In the lower ambulance parking garage at the hospital (Schuman Health Care Center on Eoarmount Avenue).

61 Beside the rooftop helipad, on the five-story building south of the V.A.J finance building.

62 Behind the middle desk inside the downtown office where you first enter in the "G-Spotlight" mission.

LITTLE HAITI

63 In a corner next to Hi-Press Gas Hot Stream ramp, behind the Moist Palms Hotel.

64 Behind Phil's Place on the corner of the bulkhead (close to the water).

65 Inside the shed at Phil's Place.

66 Down the small set of stairs, behind the building two doors down north from Kaufman Kabs.

67 Inside recessed roof of the corner building in North Haiti.

68 On the steps of the closest house on the east side of Kaufman Kabs.

69 Near the skeleton grave behind Funeraria Romero.

70 In between rooftop generators on the building connecting the north side of the Print Works (use the stairs on the north side to access the roof).

71 In a corner behind a wooden fence below the "Life's a Bitch" billboard, on the corner *east* of the Print Works.

Hidden Packages

Hyman Memorial Stadium

DOWNTOWN

LITTLE HAITI

HIDDEN PACKAGES

LITTLE HAVANA

72 Inside the Laundromat.

73 On porch of the daiquiri house that's for sale on the corner.

74 Behind the wall, across the street from Umberto's restaurant (Robina's Café).

75 On the Kaufman Kabs billboard, accessed from the adjacent building's rooftop.

76 Inside corner doughnut shop.

77 On top of the four-story building with a red awning (use the corner building's stairs to get there).

78 Upstairs in Car Showroom.

VICEPORT

79 Behind a large pipe on the ground, in the middle of the four large jet fuel tanks.

80 Between two parked tractor-trailers at the main airport parking lot.

81 In a small parking lot between the little two-story, green-and-white apartments near the shipyard.

82 Onboard the east side of the northeast Cargo ship.

83 Under Vice City Port Authority Main Building sign.

84 On southwest Cargo Ship (board the Chartered Liberty Lines using a helicopter).

85 Inside the office, deep inside the Seaplanes Tours hangar (the entrance to the hangar is on the south side, facing the water).

86 In a corner, near a fence and a building, north of 8-ball's garage at the docks.

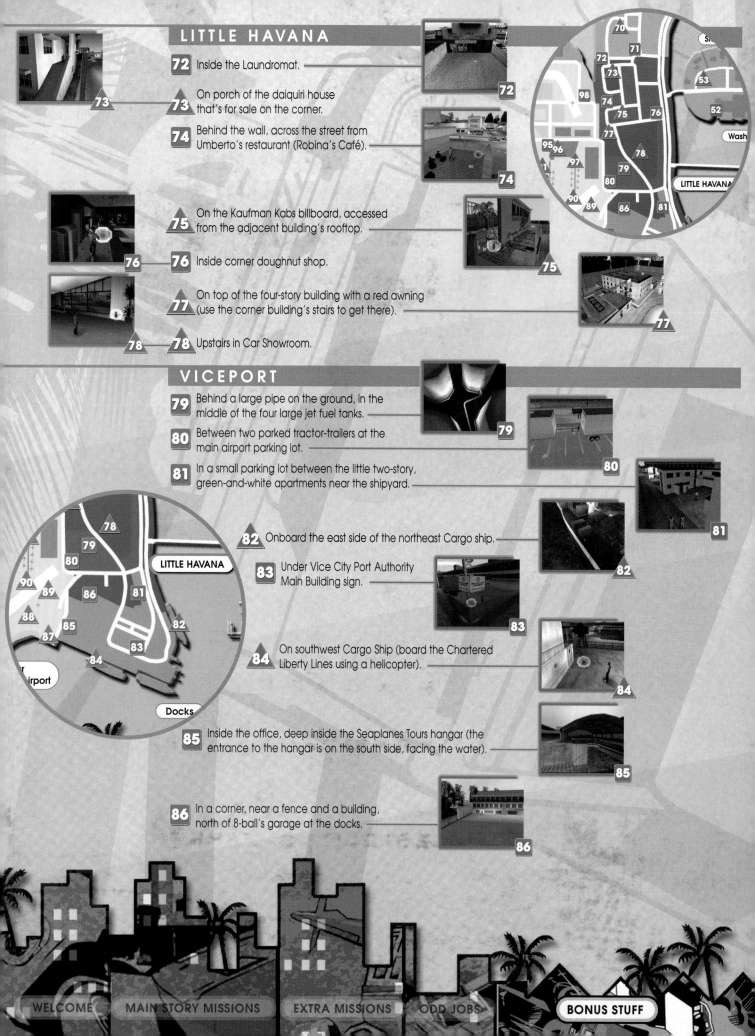

WELCOME   MAIN STORY MISSIONS   EXTRA MISSIONS   ODD JOBS   **BONUS STUFF**

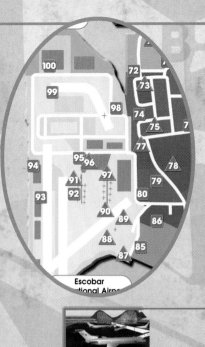

87 On top of the southeast building at the airport (Vice City International Airport Freight and Cargo Terminal).

88 On top of the southernmost helipad.

89 On top of the south McAdam Airways hangar.

90 On top, at the end of the east loading bridge.

91 On top of the southwestern-most airplane parked at the terminal.

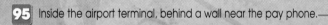

92 Under southwestern-most airplane parked at terminal.

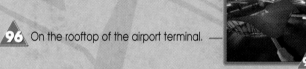

93 Under the wing of the large ROCKSTAR airplane that's poking out of the hangar.

94 Behind the Fire Station with the air traffic control tower on top of it.

95 Inside the airport terminal, behind a wall near the pay phone.

96 On the rooftop of the airport terminal.

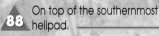

97 Top floor of Gate 8-1.

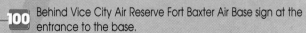

98 Behind the large collection of billboards that leads into the airport.

99 Under an airplane behind the northeast airport.

100 Behind Vice City Air Reserve Fort Baxter Air Base sign at the entrance to the base.

AUTHOR ACKNOWLEDGEMENTS

Thanks to everyone at Rockstar for giving me the Key to the Vice City and allowing me to be the first one to run wild in your new world. I would especially like to thank Devin "gangsters don't swim" Winterbottom, and Lee "I can now play the entire game with my eyes closed" Cummings. Thanks also to Phillip Marcus for your unforgettable and reputable help. Many thanks to everyone at BradyGAMES, especially David "we'll make the room" Bartley for the non-stop cell phone missions. Leigh Davis, thanks for assigning me to the best game ever. Thanks to the Angel-riding, Caddy-driving folks in Bath, NC (Jerry and Jerri Powers) for taking care of my Greenville gang while I'm away—and you, too, mom. Jennifer, I love you and I'll be on the next flight out of Vice City... just as soon as I find that hidden package at the airport.

STAFF

Publisher
David Waybright

Editor-In-Chief
H. Leigh Davis

Creative Director
Robin Lasek

Marketing Manager
Janet Eshenour

Licensing Manager
Mike Degler

Assistant Marketing Manager
Susie Nieman

CREDITS

Senior Project Editor
David B. Bartley

Screenshot Editor
Michael Owen

Lead Designer
Ann-Marie Deets

Designers
Kurt Owens
Carol Stamile
Tracy Wehmeyer